THE TEN COMMANDMENTS

Reasonable Rules for Life

Original Title: Weighed and Wanting

ANEKO PRESS

We love hearing from our readers. Please contact us at www.anekopress.com/questions-comments with any questions, comments, or suggestions.

The Ten Commandments – Dwight L. Moody

Revised Edition Copyright © 2018

First edition published 1898

Originally published by The Bible Institute Colportage Association, 829 La Salle Avenue, Chicago

Cover Design: Natalia Hawthorne

Cover Photography: Tablets, Inked Pixels/Shutterstock; Olive Branches, mickyso/Shutterstock

Editors: Sheila Wilkinson and Ruth Clark

Aneko Press

www.anekopress.com

Aneko Press, Life Sentence Publishing, and our logos are trademarks of

Life Sentence Publishing, Inc.
203 E. Birch Street
P.O. Box 652
Abbotsford, WI 54405

RELIGION / Christian Life / Spiritual Growth

Paperback ISBN: 978-1-62245-563-8

Paperback ISBN: 978-1-62245-863-9

eBook ISBN: 978-1-62245-564-5

10   9   8   7   6   5

Available where books are sold

Contents

Introduction

The Ten Commandments

Exodus 20:3-17

I. *You shall have no other gods before Me.*

II. *You shall not make for yourself an idol, or any likeness of what is in heaven above or on the earth beneath or in the water under the earth. You shall not worship them or serve them; for I, the LORD your God, am a jealous God, visiting the iniquity of the fathers on the children, on the third and the fourth generations of those who hate Me, but showing lovingkindness to thousands, to those who love Me and keep My commandments.*

III. *You shall not take the name of the LORD your God in vain, for the LORD will not leave him unpunished who takes His name in vain.*

IV. *Remember the sabbath day, to keep it holy. Six days you shall labor and do all your work, but the seventh day is a sabbath of the LORD your God; in it you shall not do any work, you* *or your son or your daughter, your male or your female servant or your cattle or your sojourner who stays with you. For in six days the LORD made the heavens and the earth, the sea and all that is in them, and rested on the seventh day; therefore the LORD blessed the sabbath day and made it holy.*

V. *Honor your father and your mother, that your days may be prolonged in the land which the LORD your God gives you.*

VI. *You shall not murder.*

VII. *You shall not commit adultery.*

VIII. *You shall not steal.*

IX. *You shall not bear false witness against your neighbor.*

X. *You shall not covet your neighbor's house; you shall not covet your neighbor's wife or his male servant or his female servant or his ox or his donkey or anything that belongs to your neighbor.*

Weighed in the Balances

In the fifth chapter of Daniel we read the history of King Belshazzar. One chapter tells us all we know about him. One short picture of his career is all we have. He bursts in upon the scene and then disappears.

We are told that Belshazzar made a great feast for a thousand of his lords and drank wine with them. In those days, a feast would sometimes last for six months in Eastern countries. How long this feast had been going on we are not told, but in the midst of it, he *gave orders to bring the gold and silver vessels which Nebuchadnezzar his father had taken out of the temple which was in Jerusalem, so that the king and his nobles, his wives and his concubines might drink from them. Then they brought the gold vessels that had been taken out of the temple, the house of God which was in Jerusalem; and the king and his nobles, his wives and his concubines drank from them. They drank the wine and praised the gods of gold and silver, of bronze, iron, wood and stone* (Daniel 5:2-4).

While this impious act was being committed, *suddenly the fingers of a man's hand emerged and began writing opposite the lampstand on the plaster of the wall of the king's palace, and the king saw the back of the hand that did the writing* (Daniel 5:5). We are not told at what hour of the day or the night it happened. Perhaps it was midnight. Perhaps nearly all the guests were more or less under the influence of drink, but they were not so drunk that they couldn't suddenly become sober, as they saw something that was supernatural – a hand writing on the wall, right over the golden candlestick.

Every face turned deathly pale. *Then the king's face grew pale and his thoughts alarmed him, and his hip joints went slack and his knees began knocking together* (Daniel 5:6). In haste, he sent for his wisest men to come and read that handwriting on the wall. They came in one after another and tried to make it out, but they could not interpret it. The king promised that whoever could read it would be made the third ruler in the kingdom and he would have gifts, and a gold chain would be put round his neck. But the wise men tried in vain. The king was greatly troubled.

At last, in the midst of his consternation, the queen came in, and she told the monarch that if he would send for one who used to interpret the dreams of Nebuchadnezzar, he could read the writing and tell him the interpretation thereof. So Daniel was sent for. He was very familiar with it. He knew his Father's handwriting.

> *Now this is the inscription that was written out: 'MENE, MENE, TEKEL, UPHARSIN.' This is the interpretation of the message: 'MENE '-God has numbered your kingdom and put an end to it. 'TEKEL '-you have been weighed on the scales and found deficient. 'PERES '-your kingdom has been divided and given over to the Medes and Persians.* (Daniel 5:25-28)

If someone had told the king an hour before that the time had come when he must step on the balances and be weighed, he would have laughed at the thought. But the vital hour had come.

The weighing was soon over. The verdict was announced, and the sentence carried out. *That same night Belshazzar the Chaldean king was slain. So Darius the Mede received the kingdom* (Daniel 5:30-31). Darius and his army came marching down those streets. There was a clash of arms. Shouts of war and victory rent the air. That night the king's blood mingled with the wine of the banquet hall. Judgment came upon him unexpectedly and suddenly; probably ninety-nine out of every hundred judgments come in this way. Death comes upon us unexpectedly; it comes upon us suddenly.

Perhaps you say, "I hope Mr. Moody is not going to compare me to that heathen king."

I tell you that a man who does evil in these gospel days is far worse than that king. We live in a land of Bibles. You can get the New Testament for a nickel, and if you don't have a nickel, you can get it for nothing. Many societies will be glad to give it to you for free. We live in the full blaze of Calvary. We live on this side of the cross, but Belshazzar lived more than five hundred years on the other side. He never heard of Jesus Christ. He never heard about the Son of God. He never heard about God except, perhaps, in connection with his father's remarkable vision. He probably had no portion of the Bible, and if he had, he probably didn't believe it. He had no godly minister to point him to the Lamb of God.

Don't tell me that you are better than that king.

I believe that he will rise in judgment and condemn many of us.

All this happened many centuries ago. Let's look at this century, this year, and ourselves. Let's come to the present time and imagine that now, while I am preaching, some balances descend from the throne of God. They are fastened to the very throne itself. It is a throne of equity and justice. You and I must be weighed. I venture to say this would be a very solemn audience. There would be no trifling. There would be no indifference. No one would be thoughtless.

Some people have their own balances. A great many are making balances to be weighed in. But after all, we must be weighed in God's balances, the balances of the sanctuary. It is a favorite thing with infidels to set their own standard and measure themselves by other people. But that will not do in the day of judgment. Now we will use God's law as a balance weight. When men find fault with the lives of professing Christians, it is a tribute to the law of God.

Tekel. It is a very short text. It is so short that I am sure you will remember it, and that is my point – to get people to remember God's own Word.

God's Handwriting

Let me call your attention to the fact that God wrote on the tables of stone at Sinai as well as on the wall of Belshazzar's palace.

These are the only messages to men that God wrote with His own hand. He wrote the commandments out twice and spoke them aloud in the hearing of Israel.

If it were known that God Himself was going to speak to man again, what eagerness and excitement there would be. For nearly nineteen hundred years, He has been silent. No inspired message has been added to the Bible for over nineteen hundred years. How eagerly all men would listen if God would speak once more. Yet men forget that the Bible is God's own Word, and that it is as truly His message today as when it was delivered long ago. The law that was given at Sinai has lost none of its solemnity. Time cannot wear out its authority or the fact of its authorship.

> Men forget that the Bible is God's own Word, and that it is as truly His message today as when it was delivered long ago.

I can imagine someone saying, "I won't be weighed by that law. I don't believe in it."

Now men may object as much as they like about other parts of the Bible, but I have never met an honest man that found fault with the Ten Commandments. Infidels may mock the Lawgiver and reject Him who has delivered us from the curse of the law, but they can't help admitting that the commandments are right. Ernest Renan said that they are for all nations and will remain the commandments of God during all the centuries.

If God created this world, He must make some laws to govern it. In order to make life safe, we must have good laws; there is not a country the sun shines upon that does not possess laws – God's law. It has come from on high, and infidels and skeptics have to admit that it is pure. Legislatures nearly all over the world adopt it as the foundation of their legal systems.

> *The law of the LORD is perfect, restoring the soul; The testimony of the LORD is sure, making wise the simple. The precepts of the LORD are right, rejoicing the heart; The commandment of the LORD is pure, enlightening the eyes* (Psalm 19:7-8).

Now the question for you and me is, are we keeping these commandments? Have we fulfilled all the requirements of the law? If God made us, as we know He did, He had a right to make that law; and if we don't use it correctly, it would have been better for us if we had never had it, for it will condemn us. We shall be found wanting. The law is all right, but are we right?

An Infidel's Testimony

The story is told of a clever infidel who sought an acquaintance about the truths of the Bible and began to read the books of Moses. He had been in the habit of sneering at the Bible, and in order to be able to refute arguments brought by Christian men, he made up his mind to read the Bible and get some idea of its contents. After he had reached the Ten Commandments, he said to a friend:

> "I will tell you what I used to think. I assumed that Moses was the leader of a horde of bandits, and having a strong mind, he acquired great influence over a superstitious people. On Mount Sinai, he lit some

sort of fireworks to the amazement of his ignorant followers, who imagined in their fear and superstition that the exhibition was supernatural. I have been looking into the nature of that law. I have been trying to see whether I could add anything to it, or take anything from it, to make it better. Sir, I cannot! It is perfect!

"The first commandment directs us to make the Creator the object of our supreme love and reverence. That is right. If He is our Creator, Preserver, and Supreme Benefactor, we ought to treat Him, and none other, as such. The second commandment forbids idolatry. That certainly is right. The third forbids profanity. The fourth fixes a time for religious worship. If there is a God, He surely should be worshipped. It is suitable that there should be an outward homage comparable to our inward regard. If God is to be worshipped, it is proper that some time should be set aside for that purpose, when all may worship Him harmoniously and without interruption. One day in seven is certainly not too much, and I do not know that it is too little.

"The fifth commandment defines the particular duties arising from family relationships. Injuries to our neighbor are then classified by the moral law. They are divided into offenses against life, chastity, property, and character; I notice that the greatest offense in each class is expressly forbidden. Thus, the greatest injury to life is murder; to chastity, adultery; to property, theft; to character, perjury. Now the greatest offense must include the least of the same kind. Murder must include every injury to life; adultery every injury to purity; and so of the rest. And the moral code is complete and perfected by a command forbidding every improper desire in regard to our neighbors.

"I have been thinking, "Where did Moses get that law?" I have read history. The Egyptians and the adjacent nations were idolaters; so were the Greeks and Romans, and the wisest or best Greeks or Romans never had a code of morals like this. Where did Moses obtain that law, which surpasses the wisdom and philosophy of the most enlightened ages? He lived in a period comparatively uncivilized, but he gave a law in which the learning and discernment of all subsequent time can detect no flaw. Where did he obtain it? He could not have been so far advanced that he devised it himself. I am satisfied with where he obtained it. It came down from heaven. It has convinced me of the truth of the religion of the Bible."

We call it the Mosaic law, but it has been correctly stated that the commandments did not originate with Moses, nor were they done away with when the Mosaic law was fulfilled in Christ, and many of its ceremonies and regulations were abolished. We can find no trace of the existence of any lawmaking body in those early times; no parliament or congress had built up a system of laws. It came to us complete and finished, and the only satisfactory account is that which tells us that God Himself wrote the commandments on tables of stone.

Binding Today

Some people seem to think we've progressed beyond the commandments. What did Christ say? *Do not think that I came to abolish the Law or the Prophets; I did not come to abolish but to fulfill. For truly I say to you, until heaven and earth pass away, not the smallest letter or stroke shall pass from the Law until all is*

> Jesus never condemned the law and the prophets, but He did condemn those who did not obey them.

accomplished. Whoever then annuls one of the least of these commandments, and teaches others to do the same, shall be called least in the kingdom of heaven; but whoever keeps and teaches them, he shall be called great in the kingdom of heaven. (Matthew 5:17-19). The commandments of God given to Moses in the Mount at Horeb are as binding today as they have ever been since the time when they were proclaimed in the hearing of the people. The Jews said the law was not given in Palestine, which belonged to Israel, but in the wilderness, because the law was for all nations.

Jesus never condemned the law and the prophets, but He did condemn those who did not obey them. Because He gave new commandments, it does not follow that He abolished the old. Christ's explanation of them made them even more far-reaching. In His Sermon on the Mount, He carried the principles of the commandments beyond the mere letter. He unfolded them and showed that they embraced more, and they are positive as well as prohibitive. The Old Testament closes with these words: *Remember the law of Moses My servant, even the statutes and ordinances which I commanded him in Horeb for all Israel. Behold, I am going to send you Elijah the prophet before the coming of the great and terrible day of the LORD. He will restore the hearts of the fathers to their children and the hearts of the children to their fathers, so that I will not come and smite the land with a curse* (Malachi 4:4-6).

Does that look as if the law of Moses was becoming obsolete?

The conviction deepens in me as the years go by that the old truths of the Bible must be stated and restated in the plainest possible language. I do not remember ever hearing a sermon preached on the commandments. I have an index of twenty-five hundred sermons preached by Spurgeon, and not one of them selects its text from the first seventeen verses of Exodus 20. The people must understand that the Ten Commandments are still binding, and there is a penalty attached to their violation. We do not want a gospel of mere sentiment.

The Sermon on the Mount did not blot out the Ten Commandments.

When Christ came, He condensed the statement of the law into this form: *You shall love the Lord your God with all your heart and with all your soul and with all your strength and with all your mind, and your neighbor as yourself* (Luke 10:27). Paul said, *Love is the fulfillment of the law* (Romans 13:10). But does this mean that the detailed precepts of the Decalogue are superseded – that they have become insignificant? Does a father cease to give children rules to obey because they love him? Does a nation burn its statute books because the people have become patriotic? Not at all. And yet people speak as if the commandments do not pertain to Christians because they have come to love God. Paul said, *Do we then nullify the Law through faith? May it never be! On the contrary, we establish the Law* (Romans 3:31). It still holds good. The commandments are necessary. As long as we obey, they do not rest heavy upon us; but as soon as we try to break away, we find they are like fences to keep us within bounds. Horses need bridles even after they have been properly broken in.

> *But we know that the Law is good, if one uses it lawfully, realizing the fact that law is not made for a righteous person, but for those who are lawless and rebellious, for the ungodly and sinners, for the unholy and profane, for those who kill their fathers or mothers, for murderers and immoral men and homosexuals and kidnappers and liars*

and perjurers, and whatever else is contrary to sound teaching. (1 Timothy 1:8-10)

Now, my friend, are you ready to be weighed by this law of God? A great many people say that if they keep the commandments, they do not need to be forgiven and saved through Christ. But have you kept them? I will admit that if you perfectly keep the commandments, you do not need to be saved by Christ; but is there a man in the whole wide world who can truly say that he has done this? Young lady, can you say, "I am ready to be weighed by the law"? Can you, young man? Will you step on the scales and be weighed one by one by the Ten Commandments?

Now face these Ten Commandments honestly and prayerfully. See if your life is right, and if you are treating God fairly. God's statutes are just, are they not? If they are right, let us see if we are right. Let us pray for the Holy Spirit to search each one of us. Let us get alone with God and read His law – read it carefully and prayerfully, and ask Him to show us our sins and what He would have us do.

Chapter 1

The First Commandment

You shall have no other gods before Me.
(Exodus 20:3)

My friend, are you ready to be weighed against this commandment? Have you fulfilled, or are you willing to fulfill, all the requirements of this law? Put it on one of the scales, and step on the other. Is your heart set upon God alone? Have you no other God? Do you love Him above father or mother, your wife, your children, home or land, wealth or pleasure?

If men were true to this commandment, obedience to the remaining nine would follow naturally. It is because they are unsound in this one that they break the others.

Feeling After God

Philosophers agree that even the most primitive races of mankind reach out beyond the world of matter to a superior Being. It is as natural for man to feel after God as it is for the ivy to feel after a support. Hunger and thirst drive him to seek for food, and there is a hunger of the soul that needs satisfying too. *O God, You are my God; I shall seek You earnestly; My soul thirsts for You, my flesh yearns for You, in a dry and weary land where there is no water* (Psalm 63:1). Man does not need to be commanded to worship, as there is not a race so high or so low in civilization that doesn't have some kind of a god. What he needs is to be directed in the right way.

The first commandment is for this purpose. Before we can worship intelligently, we must know what or whom to worship. God does not leave us in ignorance. When Paul went to Athens, he found an altar dedicated to *AN UNKNOWN GOD*, and he proceeded to tell of Him whom we worship. When God gave the commandments to Moses, He began with a declaration of His own character and demanded exclusive recognition. *I am the LORD your God, who brought you out of the land of Egypt, out of the house of slavery. "You shall have no other gods before Me"* (Exodus 20:2-3).

Dr. Dale says these words have great significance:

> The Jews knew Jehovah as the God who had held back the waves like a wall while they fled across the sea to escape the vengeance of their enemies; they knew Him as the God who had sent thunder, and lightning, and hail, plagues on cattle, and plagues on men, to punish the Egyptians and to compel them to let the children of Israel

go; they knew Him as the God whose angel
had slain the firstborn of their oppressors,
and filled the land from end to end with
death and agony and terror. He was the
same God, so Moses and Aaron told them,
who by visions and voices, in promises and
precepts, had revealed Himself long before
to Abraham, Isaac, and Jacob. We learn
what men are from what they say and from
what they do. A biography of Luther gives
a more vivid and trustworthy knowledge
of the man than the most philosophical
essay on his character and creed. The story
of his imprisonment and of his journey to
Worms, his Letters, his Sermons, and his
Table Talk are worth more than the most
elaborate speculations about him. The Jews
learned what God is, not from theologi-
cal dissertations on the Divine attributes
but from the facts of a Divine history. They
knew Him for themselves in His own acts
and His own words.[1]

Someone asked an Arab, "How do you know that there
is a God?"

"How do I know whether a man or a camel passed
my tent last night?" he replied. God's footprints in
nature and in our own experience are the best evidence
of His existence and character.

---

1   R. W. Dale, *The Ten Commandments* (London: Hodder and Stoughton, 1871), 33.

Israeli Exposure to Idols

If we remember to whom this commandment was given, we will see how necessary it was. The forefathers of the Israelites had worshipped idols not many generations prior to this. They had recently been delivered out of Egypt, a land of many gods. The Egyptians worshipped the sun, the moon, insects, and animals. The ten plagues were undoubtedly meant by God to bring confusion upon many of their sacred objects. The children of Israel were going up to take possession of a land that was inhabited by heathen who also worshipped idols. There was therefore great need of such a commandment as this. There could be no right relationship between God and man in those days any more than today, until man understood that he must recognize God alone and not offer Him a divided heart.

> The fact that God is the one and only God is a matter in which no tolerance can be shown.

If He created us, He certainly ought to have our devotion. Is it not right that He should have the first and only place in our affections?

No Compromise

The fact that God is the one and only God is a matter in which no tolerance can be shown. Religious liberty is a good thing – within certain limits. But it is one thing to show tolerance to those who agree on essentials and another to show it to those who differ on fundamental beliefs. The Romans were willing to admit any god to the Roman Pantheon. One reason the early Christians were persecuted was that they would not accept a place for Jesus Christ there. Napoleon is said to have entertained the idea of having separate temples in Paris for every known religion, so that every stranger would have a place of worship when attracted to that city. Such plans are directly opposed to the divine one. God sounded no uncertain note in this commandment. It is plain, unmistakable, and uncompromising.

We may learn a lesson from the way a farmer deals with the little shoots that spring up around the trunk of an apple tree. They look promising, and one who has not learned better might welcome their growth. But the farmer knows that they will draw the life sap from the main tree, injuring its prospects so that it will produce inferior fruit. He therefore takes his axe and his hoe and cuts away these suckers. The tree then gives a more plentiful and a finer crop.

God's Pruning Knife

You shall not is the pruning knife that God uses. From beginning to end, the Bible calls for wholehearted allegiance to Him. There is to be no compromise with other gods.

It took long years for God to impress this lesson upon the Israelites. He called them to be a chosen nation. He made them a peculiar people. But you will notice in Bible history that they continually turned away from Him and were punished with plagues, pestilence, war, and famine. Their sin was not that they renounced God altogether, but that they wanted to worship other gods besides Him. Take the case of Solomon as an example of the whole nation. He married heathen wives who turned his heart away from God and after other gods; he built high places for their idols and gave approval to their worship. That was the history of the whole nation – frequent turnings away from God, until finally He sent them into captivity in Babylon and kept them there for seventy years. Since then, the Jews have never turned to other gods.

Doesn't the church contend with the same difficulty today? There are very few who do not believe in God in their hearts, but what they will not do is give Him exclusive right-of-way. Missionaries tell us that they could easily get converts if they did not require them to be baptized, thus publicly renouncing their idols. Many people in our land would become Christians if the gate were not so straight. Christianity is too strict for them. They are not ready to promise full allegiance to God alone. Many professing Christians are stumbling blocks because their worship is divided. On Sunday, they worship God; on weekdays, God has little or no place in their thoughts.

False Gods in America

You don't have to go to heathen lands today to find false gods. America is full of them. Whatever you make most of is your god. Whatever you love more than God is your idol. Many hearts are like some Kaffirs' huts, which are so full of idols there is hardly room to turn around. Rich and poor, learned and unlearned, all classes of men and women are guilty of this sin. *Their land has also been filled with idols; They worship the work of their hands, that which their fingers have made. So the common man has been humbled and the man of importance has been abased, but do not forgive them.* (Isaiah 2:8-9).

A man may make a god of himself, a child, a mother, or some precious gift that God has given him. He may forget the Giver and let his heart go out in adoration of the gift.

Many make a god of pleasure; that is what their hearts are set on. If some old Greek or Roman came to life again and saw men in a drunken stupor, would he believe that the worship of Bacchus had died out?[2] If he saw the streets of our large cities filled with prostitutes, would he believe that the worship of Venus had ceased?[3]

Others take fashion as their god. They give their time and thought to clothes. They fear what others will think of them. Let's not flatter ourselves that all idolaters are in heathen countries.

Many people have a god of money. We haven't overcome worshipping the golden calf yet. If a man will sell his principles for gold, isn't he making it a god? If he trusts in his wealth to keep him from want and to supply his needs, aren't riches his god? Many men say, "Give me money, and I will give you heaven. What do I care for all the glories and treasures of heaven? Give me treasures here! I don't care for heaven! I want to be a successful businessman." How true are the words of Job: *If I have put my confidence in gold, and called fine gold my trust, if I have gloated because my wealth was*

---

2 Bacchus is the Roman name for Dionysus, the Greek god of wine and intoxication.

3 Venus was the goddess of love, sex, fertility, and prostitution.

great, and because my hand had secured so much; If I have looked at the sun when it shone or the moon going in splendor, and my heart became secretly enticed, and my hand threw a kiss from my mouth, that too would have been an iniquity calling for judgment, for I would have denied God above (Job 31:24-28).

But all false gods are not as deviant as these. There is the atheist who says that he does not believe in God; he denies His existence, but he can't help setting up some other god in His place. Voltaire said, "If there were no God, it would be necessary to invent him." So the atheist speaks of the Great Unknown, the First Cause, and the Infinite Mind. Then there is the deist who believes in one God who caused all things, but he doesn't believe in revelation. He only accepts such truths as can be discovered by reason. He doesn't believe in Jesus Christ or in the inspiration of the Bible. Then there is the pantheist who says, "I believe that the whole universe is God. He is in the air, the water, the sun, and the stars"; the liar and the thief are included.

Moses' Farewell Message

Let me call your attention to Deuteronomy 32:31: *Indeed their rock is not like our Rock, even our enemies themselves judge this.*

These words were uttered by Moses in his farewell address to Israel. He had been with them for forty years. He was their leader and instructor. All the blessings of heaven came to them through him. And now the old man is about to leave them. If you have never read his speech, do so. It is one of the best sermons in print. I know few sermons in the Old or New Testament that compare with it.

I can see Moses as he delivers this address. His natural activity has not declined. He still has the vigor of youth. His long, white hair flows over his shoulders, and his impressive beard covers his breast. He throws down the challenge: *Indeed their rock is not like our Rock, even our enemies themselves judge this.*

Has the human heart ever been satisfied with these false gods? Can pleasure or riches fill the soul that is empty of God? How about the atheist, the deist, the pantheist? What do they look forward to? Nothing! Man's life is full of trouble, but when the billows of affliction and disappointment rise and roll over them, they have no God to call upon. *Then shall . . . [they] cry to the gods to whom they burn incense, but they surely will not save them in the time of their disaster* (Jeremiah 11:12). Therefore, I contend that *their rock is not like our Rock.*

> Can pleasure or riches fill the soul that is empty of God?

When the hour of affliction comes, these nonbelievers call a minister to give them consolation. When I lived in Chicago, I was called out to attend many funerals. I would inquire what the deceased man believed. If I discovered he was an atheist, or a deist, or a pantheist, when I went to the funeral, they would feel insulted if in the presence of his friends I said one word about that man's doctrine. Why is it that in a trying hour, when they have been talking all the time against God, that in the darkness of affliction, they call believers in that God to administer consolation? Why doesn't the atheist preach no hereafter, no heaven, no God in the hour of affliction? This very fact is an admission that *their rock is not like our Rock, even our enemies themselves judge this.*

The deist says there is no use in praying, because nothing can change the decrees of deity; God never answers prayer. Is his rock as our Rock?

The Bible is true. There is only one God. How many men have said to me, "Mr. Moody, I would give the world if I had your faith, your consolation, the hope you have with your religion."

Isn't that proof that their rock is not as our Rock?

Some years ago I went into a man's house, but when I commenced to talk about religion, he turned to his daughter and said, "You had better leave the room. I want to say a few words to Mr. Moody." When she had gone, he opened a perfect torrent of infidelity upon me.

"Why did you send your daughter out of the room before you said this?" I asked.

"Well," he replied, "I did not think it would do her any good to hear what I said."

Is his rock as our Rock? Would he have sent his daughter out if he really believed what he said?

No Consolation except in God

No, there is no satisfaction for the soul except in the God of the Bible. We come back to Paul's words and get consolation for time and eternity: *We know that there is no such thing as an idol in the world, and that there is no God but one. For even if there are so-called gods whether in heaven or on earth, as indeed there are many gods and many lords, yet for us there is but one God, the Father, from whom are all things and we exist for Him; and one Lord, Jesus Christ, by whom are all things, and we exist through Him* (1 Corinthians 8:4-6).

My friend, can you say that sincerely? Is all your hope centered on God in Christ? Are you trusting Him alone? Are you ready to step on the scales and be weighed against this first commandment?

Wholehearted Allegiance

God will not accept a divided heart. He must be your absolute monarch. There is not room in your heart for two thrones. Christ said, *No one can serve two masters; for either he will hate the one and love the other, or he will be devoted to one and despise the other. You cannot serve God and wealth* (Matthew 6:24). Notice He did not say, "No man *shall* serve . . . Ye *shall* not serve," but rather, *No one can serve . . . Ye cannot serve.* That is more than a command; it means that you cannot mix the worship of the true God with the worship of another god any more than you can mix oil and water. It cannot be done. There is not room for any other throne in the heart if Christ is there. If worldliness should come in, godliness would go out.

The road to heaven and the road to hell lead in different directions. Which master will you choose to follow? Be an out-and-out Christian. *And serve Him only* (Matthew 4:10). Only in this way can you be well pleasing to God. The Jews were punished with seventy years of captivity because they worshipped false gods. They have suffered nearly nineteen hundred years because they rejected the Messiah. Will you incur God's displeasure by rejecting Christ too? He died to save you. Trust Him with your whole heart, *For with the heart a person believes, resulting in righteousness* (Romans 10:10).

I believe that when Christ has first place in our hearts, when the kingdom of God is first in everything, we will have power, and we will not have power until we give Him His rightful place. If we let some false god come in and steal our love away from the God of heaven, we will have no peace or power.

Chapter 2

The Second Commandment

You shall not make for yourself an idol, or any likeness of what is in heaven above or on the earth beneath or in the water under the earth. You shall not worship them or serve them; for I, the LORD your God, am a jealous God, visiting the iniquity of the fathers on the children, on the third and the fourth generations of those who hate Me, but showing lovingkindness to thousands, to those who love Me and keep My commandments. (Exodus 20:4-6)

The first commandment, which we have just considered, points out the one true object of worship; this second commandment tells us the right way to worship. The former commands us to worship God alone; this one calls for purity and spirituality as we approach Him. The former condemns the worship of false gods; this one prohibits false forms. It relates more to outward acts of worship, but these are only expressions of what is in the heart.

Perhaps you will say that you have no trouble with this. We might go off to other ages or other lands and find people who make images and bow down to them, but we have no images here. Let's see if this is true. Let's step on the scales and see how we weigh when measured against this commandment.

I believe this is where the battle is fought. Satan tries to keep us from worshipping God correctly and from making Him first in everything. If I let some image made by man get into my heart and take the place of God the Creator, it is a sin. I believe that Satan is willing to have us worship anything, however sacred – the Bible, the crucifix, the church – if only we do not worship God Himself.

> Satan tries to keep us from worshipping God correctly and from making Him first in everything.

You cannot find a place in the Bible where a man has been allowed to bow down and worship anyone but the God of heaven and Jesus Christ, His Son. In the book of Revelation, when an angel came down to John, he was about to fall down and worship him, but the angel would not let him. If an angel from heaven is not to be worshipped, then when you find people bowing down to pictures or images, even when they bow down to worship the cross, *it is a sin.* There are a great many who seem to be carried away with these things. *You shall have no other gods before me. You shall not bow down to them* [graven images]. God wants us to worship Him only, and if we do not believe that Jesus Christ is God manifest in the flesh, we should not worship Him. But I have no more doubt about the divinity of Christ than I have that I exist.

Worship involves two things: the internal belief and the external act. We transgress in our hearts before we ever give a public expression by having a wrong concept of God and of Jesus Christ. As someone has said, it is wrong to have degenerate opinions as well as to be guilty of degenerate practices. That is what Paul meant when he said, *We ought not to think that the Divine Nature is like gold or silver or stone, an image formed by the art and thought of man* (Acts 17:29). The opinions that some people hold about Christ are not in accordance with the Bible and are real violations of this second commandment.

A Question

The question at once arises, is this commandment intended to forbid the use of drawings and pictures of created things altogether? Some contend that it does. They point to the Jews and the Mohammedans as proof. The Jews have never been inclined toward art. The Mohammedans to this day do not use designs of animals in patterns. I do not agree with them. I think God only meant to forbid images and other representations when these were intended to be used as objects of religious veneration. *You shall not make for yourself . . . You shall not worship them or serve them.* In Exodus we are told that God ordered the bowls of the golden candlestick for the tabernacle to be made *like almond blossoms with a bulb and a flower* (Exodus 25:33); and the robe of the ephod had a hem on which they were to put a bell and a pomegranate alternately (Exodus 29:25). How could God order something that broke this second commandment?

I believe that this commandment is a call for spiritual worship. It is in line with Christ's declaration to that Samaritan woman: *God is spirit, and those who worship Him must worship in spirit and truth* (John 4:24).

This is precisely what is difficult for men to do. The apostles were hardly in their graves before the people began to put up images of them and to worship relics. People have a desire for something tangible, something that they can see. It is so much easier to live in the sense than in the spirit. That is why there is a demand for ritualism. Some people are born Puritans; they want a simple form of worship. Others think they cannot get along without forms and ceremonies that appeal to the senses. And many whose hearts are not sincere before God take refuge in these forms and ease their consciences by making an outward show of religion. The second commandment restrains this desire and tendency.

God is grieved when we are untrue to Him. God is love, and He is wounded when our affections are transferred to anything else. The penalty attached to this commandment teaches us that man reaps what he sows, whether good or bad; and not only that, but his children will also reap with him. Notice that punishment is visited upon the children unto the third and the fourth generations, while mercy is shown unto thousands, or (as it is more correctly translated) unto the thousandth generation.

The Folly of Images

Think for a moment, and you will see how useless it is to try to make any representation of God. Christians have tried to paint the Trinity, but how can you depict the invisible? Can you draw a picture of your own soul or spirit or will? Moses impressed this upon Israel that when God spoke to them out of the midst of the fire, they saw no similarity but only heard His voice.

A picture or image of God degrades our concept of Him. It fastens us down to one idea, whereas we ought to grow in grace and in knowledge. It makes God finite. It brings Him down to our level and has given rise to the horrible idols of India and China, because they fashion these images according to their own notions. How would the president feel if Americans made such hideous objects to resemble him as people make of their gods in heathen countries? Isaiah denounced with tremendous irony the folly of idol makers, the smith who fashioned gods with tongs and hammers, the carpenter who took a tree and used part of it for a fire to warm himself and roast his meat, and made part of it in the figure of a man with his rule and plane and compass and called it his god and worshipped it.

> A picture or image of God degrades our concept of Him.

> *Then it becomes something for a man to burn,*
> *so he takes one of them and warms himself;*
> *he also makes a fire to bake bread. He also*
> *makes a god and worships it; he makes it a*
> *graven image and falls down before it. Half*
> *of it he burns in the fire; over this half he*
> *eats meat as he roasts a roast and is satis-*
> *fied. He also warms himself and says, "Aha!*
> *I am warm, I have seen the fire." But the rest*
> *of it he makes into a god, his graven image.*
> *He falls down before it and worships; he also*
> *prays to it and says, "Deliver me, for you are*
> *my god."* (Isaiah 44:15-17).

A man must be greater than anything he is able to make or manufacture. How foolish then to think of worshipping such things!

The tendency of the human heart to represent God by something that appeals to the senses is the origin of all idolatry. It leads directly to idol worship. At first, there may be no desire to worship the thing itself, but it inevitably ends in that. As Dr. MacLaren says, "Enlisting the senses as the allies of the spirit in worship is risky work. They are very apt to fight for their own hand when they once begin, and the history of all symbolic and ceremonial worship shows that the experiment is much more likely to end in sensualizing religion than in spiritualizing sense."[4]

---

4   Alexander Maclaren (1826-1910), *The Epistles of St. Paul to the Colossians and Philemon.*

Pictures and Images

But someone might say, "I find pictures and images are a great help to me. I know that they are not themselves sacred, but they help me in my devotions to fix my thoughts on God."

When Dr. Trumbull was in Northfield, he used an illustration that is a good answer to this. He said:

> Suppose a young man was watching from a window for his absent mother's return, hoping to catch the first glimpse of her approaching face. Would he be wise or foolish in putting up a photograph of her on the window frame before him as a help to bring her as he watched? As there can be no doubt about the answer to that question, so there can be no doubt that we can come into communion with God best by closing our eyes to everything that can be seen with the natural eye and opening the eyes of our spirit to the sight of God the Spirit.

I'd rather have five minutes' communion with Christ than spend years before pictures and images of Him. Whatever comes between my soul and my Maker is not a help to me but a hindrance. God has given different means of grace by which we can approach Him. Let's use these and not seek for other things that He has distinctly forbidden.

Dr. Dale says that in his college days he had an engraving of our Lord hanging over his mantelpiece.

> The calmness, the dignity, the gentleness,

and the sadness of the face represented the
highest conceptions which I had in those
days of the human presence of Christ. I
often looked at it and seldom without being
touched by it. I discovered in the course of a
few months that the superstitious sentiments
were gradually clustering about it, which are
always created by the visible representations
of the Divine. The engraving was becoming
the shrine of God manifest in the flesh to
me, and I understood the growth of idolatry.
The visible symbol is at first a symbol and
nothing more; it assists thought; it stirs passion. In the end it is identified with the God
whom it represents. If I bow before a crucifix
in prayer every day, if I address it as though
it were Christ, though I know it is not, I shall
come to feel a reverence and love for it which
are of the very essence of idolatry.

Did you ever stop to think that the world doesn't have a
single picture of Christ that has been handed down to
us from His disciples? Who knows what He was like?
The Bible does not tell us how He looked except in one
or two isolated general expressions, as when it says, *so
His appearance was marred more than any man and
His form more than the sons of men* (Isaiah 52:14). We
don't know anything definite about His features, the
color of His hair and eyes, and the other details that
would help to give a true representation. What artist
can tell us? He left no keepsakes to His disciples. His

clothes were seized by the Roman soldiers who crucified Him. Not a solitary thing was left to be handed down among His followers. Doesn't it look as if Christ left no relics so they wouldn't be held sacred and worshipped?

History tells us further that the early Christians shrank from making pictures and statues of any kind of Christ. They knew Him as they had seen Him after His resurrection, and they had promises of His continued presence that pictures could not make any more real.

Jesus left no keepsakes to His disciples.

I have seen very few pictures of Christ that do not more or less repel me. I sometimes think that it is wrong to have pictures of Him at all.

Speaking of the crucifix, Dr. Dale says:

> It makes our worship and prayer unreal.
> We are adoring a Christ who does not
> exist. He is not on the cross now but on the
> throne. His agonies are passed forever. He
> has risen from the dead. He is at the right
> hand of God. If we pray to a dying Christ,
> we are not praying to Christ but to a mere
> remembrance of Him. The injury that the
> crucifix has inflicted on the religious life of
> Christendom by encouraging a morbid and
> unreal devotion is incalculable. It has given
> us a dying Christ instead of a living Christ,
> a Christ separated from us by many centu-
> ries instead of a Christ nigh at hand.[5]

---

5   R. W. Dale, *The Ten Commandments* (London: Hoddard and
     Stoughton, 1871), 49.

The Indwelling Christ

No one can say that we have a need for such things today. *Behold, I stand at the door and knock; if anyone hears My voice and opens the door, I will come in to him and will dine with him, and he with Me* (Revelation 3:20). If Christ is in our hearts, why do we need to set Him before our eyes? *For where two or three have gathered together in My name, I am there in their midst* (Matthew 18:20). If we take hold of that promise by faith, what need is there of outward symbols and reminders? If the King Himself is present, why do we need to bow down before statues that are supposed to represent Him? To fill His place with an image (someone has said) is like blotting the sun out of the heavens and substituting some other light in its place. "You cannot see Him through chinks of ceremonialism or through the blind eyes of erring man or by images carved and sculptured with art and man's work, or in cunningly devised fables of artificial and perverted theology. No, seek Him in His own Word, in the revelation of Himself, which He gives to all who walk in His ways. So you will be able to keep that admonition of the last word of all the New Testament revelation: *Little children, guard yourselves from idols* (1 John 5:21)."

I believe many earnest Christians would be found lacking if put on the balances against this commandment. *Tekel* is the sentence that would be written against them, because their worship of God and of Christ is not pure. May God open our eyes to the danger that is creeping more and more into public worship throughout Christendom! Let us ever bear in mind

Christ's words in the fourth chapter of John's gospel, which show that true spiritual worship is not a matter of special times and special places because it is for all times and all places:

> *Believe Me, an hour is coming when neither in this mountain nor in Jerusalem will you worship the Father. But an hour is coming, and now is, when the true worshipers will worship the Father in spirit and truth; for such people the Father seeks to be His worshipers. God is spirit, and those who worship Him must worship in spirit and truth.* (John 4:21, 23-24)

Chapter 3

The Third Commandment

You shall not take the name of the LORD your God in vain, for the LORD will not leave him unpunished who takes His name in vain. (Exodus 20:7)

I was amazed not long ago when talking to a man who thought he was a Christian to find that once in a while, when he got angry, he would swear. I said, "My friend, I don't see how you can tear down with one hand what you are trying to build up with the other. I don't see how you can profess to be a child of God and let those words come out of your lips."

He replied, "Mr. Moody, if you knew me you would understand. I have a very quick temper. I inherited it from my father and mother, and it is uncontrollable; but my swearing comes only from the lips."

When God said He *will not leave him unpunished who takes His name in vain*, He meant what He said, and I don't believe anyone can be a true child of God who takes the name of God in vain. What is the grace of God for, if it is not to give me control of my temper so I won't lose control and bring the curse of God upon myself? When a man is born of God, God takes the "swear" out of him. Make the fountain good, and the stream will be good. Let the heart be right, and then the language will be right, and the whole life will be right. But no man can serve God and keep His law until he is born of God. There we see the necessity of the new birth.

To take God's name *in vain* means either (1) lightly, without thinking, flippantly, or (2) profanely, deceitfully.

Using God's Name Irreverently

I think it is shocking to use God's name with so little reverence as is common today, even among professing Christians. We are told that the Jews held His name so sacred that the covenant name of God was never mentioned among them except once a year by the high priest on the Day of Atonement, when he went into the holy of holies. What a contrast that is to the familiar use Christians make of it in public and private worship! We are apt to rush into God's presence and rush out again without any real sense of the reverence and awe that is due Him. We forget that we are on holy ground.

Do you know how often the word *reverend* occurs in the Bible? Only once. And what is it used in connection with? God's name. Psalm 111:9 JUB says, *Holy and reverend is his name.* So important did the Jewish rabbis consider this commandment that they said the whole world trembled when it was first proclaimed on Sinai.

Using God's Name Profanely

But though there is far too much frivolous, familiar use of God's name, the commandment is broken a great deal more by profanity. Taking the name of God in vain is blasphemy. Is there a swearing man who is reading this? What would you do if you were put on the balances of the sanctuary, if you had to step on opposite to this third commandment? Think a moment. Have you been taking God's name in vain today?

I do not believe men would ever have been guilty of swearing unless God had forbidden it. They do not swear by their friends, their fathers or mothers, their wives or children. They want to show how they despise God's law.

Many men think there is nothing in swearing. Bear in mind that God sees something wrong in it, and He says He will not hold men guiltless, even though society does.

I met a man one time who told me he had never sinned in his life. He was the first perfect man I had ever met. I decided to question him and began to measure him by the law. I asked him, "Do you ever get angry?"

"Well," he said, "sometimes I do, but I have a right to do so. It is righteous indignation."

"Do you swear when you get angry?" He admitted he did sometimes. "Then," I asked, "are you ready to meet God?"

"Yes," he replied, "because I never mean anything when I swear."

Suppose I steal a man's watch and he comes after me. "Yes," I say, "I stole your watch and pawned it, but I did not mean anything by it. I pawned it and spent the money, but I did not mean anything by it."

You would laugh at such a statement.

Ah, friends! You cannot trifle with God in that way. Even if you swear without meaning it, it is forbidden by God. Christ said, *Every careless word that people speak, they shall give an accounting for it in the day of judgment. For by your words you will be justified, and by your words you will be condemned* (Matthew 12:36-37). You will be held accountable whether your words are idle or blasphemous.

A Senseless Habit

The habit of swearing is condemned by all sensible persons. It has been called the most unnecessary and unjustified sin, because no one gains by it; it is not only sinful, but also useless. An old writer said that when the accusing angel, who records men's words, flies up to heaven with an oath, he blushes as he hands it in.

When a man blasphemes, he shows an utter contempt for God. I was in the army during the war and heard men cursing and swearing.[6] Some godly woman would pass along the ranks looking for her wounded son and not an oath would be heard. They would not

---

6   D. L. Moody served as chairman of the Christian Commission in the Civil War and went to camps and battlefields and distributed Bibles, hymnbooks, and prayer books.

swear before their mothers, their wives, or their sisters; they had more respect for them than they had for God!

Isn't it a terrible condemnation that swearing continued until it came to be recognized as a vulgar thing, a sin against society? Men dropped it then – men who never thought of its being a sin against God.

There will be no swearing men in the kingdom of God. They will have to drop that sin and repent of it before they see the kingdom of God.

How to Keep from Swearing

Men often ask, "How can I keep from swearing?"

I will tell you. If God puts His love into your heart, you will have no desire to curse Him. If you have much regard for God, you will no more think of cursing Him than you would think of speaking lightly or disparagingly of a mother whom you love. But the natural man is at enmity with God and has utter contempt for His law. When that law is written on his heart, there will be no trouble in obeying it.

> There will be no swearing men in the kingdom of God.

When I was out west about thirty years ago, I was preaching in the open air one day, when a man drove up in a fine carriage. After listening a little while to what I was saying, he put the whip to his fine-looking horse and away he went. I never expected to see him again, but the next night he came back, and he kept on coming night after night.

I noticed that his forehead itched. You have probably noticed people who keep putting their hands to their foreheads – he didn't want anyone to see him shedding tears. After all, it is not a manly thing to shed tears in a religious meeting.

After the meeting, I said to a gentleman, "Who is that man who drives up here every night? Is he interested?"

"Interested! I should think not! You should have heard the way he talked about you today."

"Well," I said, "that is a sign he is interested."

If no man ever has anything to say against you, your Christianity isn't worth much. Men said of John the Baptist, the forerunner of Jesus, *He has a demon*, and Jesus said that *if they have called the head of the house Beelzebul, how much more will they malign the members of his household?* (Matthew 11:18; 10:25).

I asked where this man lived, but my friend told me not to go see him, for he would only curse me. I said, "It takes God to curse a man; man can only bring curses on his own head." I found out where he lived and went to see him. He was the wealthiest man within a hundred miles of that place and had a wife and seven beautiful children. Just as I arrived at his gate, I saw him coming out of the front door. I stepped up to him and said, "You are Mr. ___, I believe?"

He said, "Yes, sir, that is my name." Then he straightened up and asked, "What do you want?"

"Well," I said, "I would like to ask you a question, if you won't be angry."

"Well, what is it?"

"I am told that God has blessed you above all men in this part of the country; that He has given you wealth, a beautiful Christian wife, and seven lovely children.

I do not know if it is true, but I hear that all He gets in return is cursing and blasphemy."

He said, "Come in, come in." I went in. "Now," he said, "what you said out there is true. If any man has a fine wife, I am the man, and I have a lovely family of children. God has been good to me. But do you know, we had company here the other night, and I cursed my wife at the table and did not realize it until after the company had gone. I never felt so mean and contemptible in my life as when my wife told me about it. She said she wanted the floor to open and let her down out of her seat. If I have tried once, I have tried a hundred times to stop swearing. You preachers don't know anything about it."

"Yes," I said, "I know all about it; I have been a drummer."

"But," he said, "you don't know anything about a businessman's troubles. When he is harassed and tormented the whole time, he can't help swearing."

"Oh, yes," I said, "he can. I know something about it. I used to swear myself."

"What! You used to swear?" he asked. "How did you stop?"

"I never stopped."

"Why, you don't swear now, do you?"

"No, I have not sworn for years."

"How did you stop?"

"I never stopped. It stopped itself."

He said, "I don't understand this."

"No," I said, "I know you don't. But I came up to

talk to you, so that you will never want to swear again as long as you live."

I told him how Christ in the heart would take the temptation to swear out of a man.

"Well," he said, "how am I to get Christ?"

"Get right down here and tell Him what you want."

"But," he said, "I was never on my knees in my life. I have been cursing all my days, and I don't know how to pray or what to pray for."

"Well," I said, "it is mortifying to have to call on God for mercy when you have never used His name except in oaths, but He will not turn you away. Ask God to forgive you if you want to be forgiven."

Then the man got down and prayed – only a few sentences, but thank God, it is the short prayers, after all, which bring the quickest answers. After he prayed, he got up and said, "What shall I do now?"

I said, "Go down to the church and tell the people there that you want to be an out-and-out Christian."

"I cannot do that," he said. "I never go to church except to some funeral."

"Then it is high time for you to go for something else," I said.

After a while he promised to go, but he did not know what the people would say. At the next church prayer meeting, the man was there, and I sat right in front of him. He stood up and put his hands on the bench, and he trembled so much that I could feel the bench shake. He said, "My friends, you know all about me. If God can save a wretch like me, I want to have you pray for my salvation."

That was thirty-odd years ago. Sometime ago I was back in that town and did not see him, but when I was in California, a man invited me to dinner with him. I told him that I could not do so, for I had another engagement. Then he asked if I remembered him and told me his name. "Oh," I said, "tell me, have you ever sworn since that night you knelt in your den and asked God to forgive you?"

"No," he replied, "I have never had a desire to swear since then. It was all taken away."

He was not only converted, but he had also become an earnest, active Christian, and all these years he has been serving God. That is what will take place when a man is born of the divine nature.

Is there a swearing man ready to put this commandment on the scales and be weighed? Suppose you swear only once in six months or a year; suppose you swear only once in ten years; do you think God will hold you guiltless for that act? It shows that your heart is not clean in God's sight. What are you going to do, blasphemer? Would you not be found deficient? You would be like a feather in the balance.

Chapter 4

The Fourth Commandment

*Remember the sabbath day, to keep it holy.
Six days you shall labor and do all your
work, but the seventh day is a sabbath of the
LORD your God; in it you shall not do any
work, you or your son or your daughter, your
male or your female servant or your cattle
or your sojourner who stays with you. For
in six days the LORD made the heavens and
the earth, the sea and all that is in them,
and rested on the seventh day; therefore the
LORD blessed the sabbath day and made it
holy.* (Exodus 20:8-11)

During the last twenty-five years, there has been a weakening in this country with regard to the Sabbath, and many men have lost spiritual power like Samson, because they are not solid on this question. Can you say that you observe the Sabbath properly?

You may be a professed Christian; are you obeying this commandment? Or do you neglect the house of God on the Sabbath day and spend your time drinking and carousing in places of vice and crime, showing contempt for God and His law? Are you ready to step on the scales? Where were you last Sabbath? How did you spend it?

I honestly believe that this commandment is just as binding today as it ever was. I have talked with men who have said that it has been abolished, but they have never been able to point to any place in the Bible where God repealed it. When Christ was on earth, He did nothing to set it aside; He freed it from the traces under which the scribes and Pharisees had put it and gave it its true place. *The Sabbath was made for man, and not man for the Sabbath* (Mark 2:27). It is just as practical and necessary for men today as it ever was – in fact, more than ever, because we live in such an intense age.

The Sabbath was binding in Eden, and it has been in force ever since. This fourth commandment begins with the word *remember*, showing that the Sabbath already existed when God wrote this law on the tables of stone at Sinai. How can men claim that this one commandment has been done away with when they will admit that the other nine are still binding?

I believe that the Sabbath question today is a vital one for the whole country. It is the burning question of the present time. If you give up the Sabbath, the church goes with it; if you give up the church, the home goes; and if the home goes, the nation goes. That is the direction we are traveling in.

The church of God is losing its power because many people are giving up the Sabbath and using that day to promote selfishness.

How to Observe the Sabbath

Sabbath means "rest," and the meaning of the word gives a hint as to the true way to observe the day. God rested after creation and ordained the Sabbath as a rest for man. He blessed it and sanctified it. "Remember *the rest day* to keep it *holy*." It is the day when the body may be refreshed and strengthened after six days of labor, and the soul can be drawn into closer fellowship with its Maker.

True observance of the Sabbath may be considered under two general heads: cessation from ordinary secular work and commencement of religious exercises.

Cessation from Secular Work

A man ought to turn aside from his ordinary employment one day in seven. There are many whose occupations will not permit them to observe Sunday, but they should observe some other day as a Sabbath. Saturday is my day of rest because I generally preach on Sunday, and I look forward to it as a boy does to a holiday. God knows what we need.

Ministers and missionaries often tell me that they take no rest day; they do not need it because they are in the Lord's work. That is a mistake. When God was giving Moses instructions about the building of the tabernacle, He referred to the Sabbath and gave injunctions for its strict observance. Later, when Moses was conveying the words of the Lord to the children of Israel, he interpreted them by saying that not even sticks were to be gathered on the Sabbath to kindle fires for smelting or other purposes. In spite of their zeal and haste to erect the tabernacle, the workmen were to have their day of rest. The command applies to ministers and others engaged in Christian work today as much as to those Israelite workmen of old.

Works of Necessity and Emergency
In judging whether any work may or may not be lawfully done on the Sabbath, we must consider the reason and objective for doing it. Exceptions are to be made for works of necessity and works of emergency. By *works of necessity* I mean those acts that Christ justified when He approved of leading one's ox or ass to water. Watchmen, police, stokers onboard steamers, and many others have engagements that necessitate their working on the Sabbath. By *works of emergency* I mean those referred to by Christ when He approved of pulling an ox or an ass out of a pit on the Sabbath day. In case of fire or sickness, a man is often called on to do things that would not otherwise be justifiable.

A Christian man was once urged by his employer to work on Sunday. "Doesn't your Bible say that if your ass falls into a pit on the Sabbath, you may pull him out?"

"Yes," replied the other, "but if the ass had the habit of falling into the same pit every Sabbath, I would either fill the pit or sell the ass."

Every man must settle the question with his own conscience.

No man should make another man work seven days in the week. One day is demanded for rest. A man who has to work the seven days has nothing to look forward to, and life becomes humdrum. Many Christians are guilty in this respect.

Sabbath Traveling

Take, for instance, the question of Sabbath traveling. I believe we are breaking God's laws by using public transportation on Sunday and depriving drivers and others of their Sabbath. Remember the fourth commandment expressly refers to the *stranger that is within your gates*. Doesn't that include Sabbath travel?

But you ask, "What are we to do? How are we to get to church?"

> A man who has to work the seven days has nothing to look forward to, and life becomes humdrum.

I reply, "On foot." It will be better for you. Once when I was holding meetings in London, in my ignorance I made arrangements to preach four times in different places one Sabbath. After I had made the appointments, I found I had to walk sixteen miles; but I walked it, and I slept that night with a clear conscience. I have made it a rule never to use public transportation, and if I have access to a private car, I insist that the man rest on Monday. I want no cab driver to rise up in judgment against me.

My friends, if we want to help keep the Sabbath, don't allow businessmen and Christians to use public transportation on the Sabbath. I would hate to own stock in those companies and be the means of taking the Sabbath from these men and have to answer for it at the day of judgment. Let those who are Christians endeavor to keep a clear conscience on this point.

Business on the Sabbath

There are many who are inclined to use the Sabbath to make money. This is no new sin. The prophet Amos hurled his invectiveness against oppressors who said, *When will the new moon be over, so that we may sell grain, and the Sabbath, that we may open the wheat market, to make the bushel smaller and the shekel bigger, and to cheat with dishonest scales* (Amos 8:5).

Covetous men have always chafed under the restraint, but not until the present time do we find that they have openly counted on Sabbath trade to make money. We are told that many companies would not make a profit if it were not for the Sabbath business, and the Sabbath edition of newspapers is also considered the most profitable.

The railroad men of this country are breaking down from stress and fatigue and dying at the age of fifty or sixty. They think their business is so important that they must run their trains seven days a week. Businessmen travel on the Sabbath to be ready for business on Monday morning. But if they do this, God will not prosper them.

Work is good for man, and it is commanded, *Six days you shall labor*; but overwork and work on the Sabbath takes away the best thing he has.

Necessary and Beneficial

The good effect on a nation's health and happiness produced by the return of the Sabbath with its cessation from work cannot be overestimated. It is needed to repair and restore the body after six days of work. It is proved that a man can do more in six days than in seven. Lord Beaconsfield said, "Of all divine institutions, the most divine is that which secures a day of rest for man. I hold it to be the most valuable blessing conceded to man. It is the cornerstone of all civilization, and its removal might affect even the health of the people." Mr. Gladstone recently told a friend that the secret of his long life was that, amid all the pressure of public cares, he never forgot the Sabbath with its rest for the body and the soul. The Constitution of the United States protects the president in his weekly day of rest. He has ten days, "Sundays excepted," in which to consider a bill that has been sent to him for signature. Every workingman in the republic ought to be as thoroughly protected as the president is. If workingmen participated in a strike against unnecessary work on the Sabbath, they would have the sympathy of a good many people.

"Our bodies are seven-day clocks," says Talmage, "and they need to be wound up, and if they are not wound up, they run down into the grave. No man can continuously break the Sabbath and keep his physical and mental health. Ask aged men, and they will tell you they never knew men who continuously broke the Sabbath, who did not fail in mind, body, or moral principles."

All that has been said about rest for man is true for working animals also. God didn't forget them in this commandment, and man should not forget them either.

Religious Activity

But *rest* does not mean idleness. No man enjoys idleness for any length of time. When a man goes on a vacation, he does not lie around doing nothing all the time. Hard work at tennis, hunting, and other pursuits fills the hours. A healthy mind must find something to do.

Hence, the Sabbath rest does not mean inactivity. "Satan finds some mischief still for idle hands to do."[7] The best way to avoid bad thoughts and temptation is to engage in active religious exercises.

In regard to these activities, we should avoid extremes. On the one hand, we should resist a rigorous Sabbath observance that is not commanded in Scripture but reminds one of the formalism of the Pharisees more than of the spirit of the gospel. Such strictness does more harm than good. It repels people and makes the Sabbath a burden. On the other hand, we should jealously guard against a loose way of keeping the Sabbath. Already in many cities it is openly disrespectful.

> The best way to avoid bad thoughts and temptation is to engage in active religious exercises.

When I was a boy, the Sabbath lasted from sundown on Saturday to sundown on Sunday, and I remember how we boys used to shout when it was over. It was the

---

7   Isaac Watts (1675-1750), from the poem "How Doth the Little Busy Bee."

worst day in the week for us. I believe it can be made the brightest day in the week. Every child should be raised so that he and his friend can say they would rather have the other six days weeded out of their memory than the Sabbath of their childhood.

Public Worship

Make the Sabbath a day of religious activity. First, of course, is attendance at public worship. "There is a discrepancy," says John McNeill, "between our creed about the sabbath day and our actual conduct. In many families, at ten o'clock on the sabbath, attendance at church is still an open question. There is no open question on Monday morning – 'John, will you go to work today?'"

A minister rebuked a farmer for not attending church, and said, "You know, John, you are never absent from the market."

"Oh," was the reply, "we must go to market."

Someone has said that without the Sabbath the church of Christ could not exist on earth as a visible organization. Another has said, "We need to be in the drill of observance as well as in the liberty of faith." Human nature is so treacherous that we are apt to omit things altogether unless there is some special reason for doing them. A man is not likely to worship at all unless he has regularly appointed times and means for worship. Family and private devotions are almost certain to be omitted altogether, unless one gets into the habit and has a special time set apart daily.

A Remembrance

I blamed my mother for sending me to church on the Sabbath. On one occasion, the preacher had to send someone to the balcony to wake me up. I thought it was hard to have to work in the field all week and then be obliged to go to church and hear a sermon I didn't understand. I didn't think I'd go to church anymore when I left home, but I had such a habit of going that I couldn't stay away. After one or two Sabbaths of being away, back again to the house of God I went. I first found Christ there, and I have often said, "Mother, I thank you for making me go to the house of God when I didn't want to go."

Parents, if you want your children to grow up and honor you, have them honor the Sabbath day. Don't let them go off fishing and hang with bad company, or before long they will come home and curse you. I know few things more beautiful than to see a father and mother coming up the aisle with their daughters and sons and sitting down together to hear the Word of God. It is a good thing to have the children not in some remote loft or balcony, but in a good, prominent place. Though they cannot understand the sermon now, when they get older, they won't desire to break away; they will continue attending public worship in the house of God.

But we must not mistake the means for the end. We must not think that the Sabbath is just for the sake of being able to attend meetings. Some people think they must spend the whole day at meetings or private devotions. The result is that at nightfall they are tired out, and the day has brought them no rest. The number of church services attended ought to be measured by the person's ability to enjoy them and get good from them without being wearied. Attending meetings is not the only way to observe the Sabbath. The Israelites were commanded to keep the Sabbath in their dwellings as well as in their assemblies. The home, that center of great influence over the life and character of the people, ought to be made the focal point of true Sabbath observance.

Home Observance

Jeremiah classified godless families with the heathen: *Pour out Your wrath on the nations that do not know You and on the families that do not call Your name; For they have devoured Jacob; They have devoured him and consumed him and have laid waste his habitation* (Jeremiah 10:25).

Many mothers have written to me at one time or another for suggestions on how to entertain their children on the Sabbath. The boys say, "I do wish 'twas night," or, "I do hate the Sabbath," or, "I do wish the Sabbath was over." It ought to be the happiest day in the week for them, one to be looked forward to with pleasure. Many suggestions might be followed to make this happen. Make family prayers especially attractive by having the children learn some verse or story from the Bible. Give more time to your children than you can give on weekdays; read to them and perhaps take them for a walk in the afternoon or evening. Show by your conduct that the Sabbath is a delight, and they will soon catch your spirit. Set aside some time for religious instruction without making this a task. You can make it interesting for the children by telling Bible stories and asking them to guess the names of the characters. Have Sunday games for the younger children. Picture books and puzzle maps of Palestine can be easily obtained. Sunday music and Sunday clocks are other devices. Set aside attractive books that are strictly for the Sabbath. By doing this, the children can be brought to look forward to the day with eagerness and pleasure.

Private Observance

Apart from public and family observance, the individual should devote a portion of the time to his own edification. Prayer, meditation, and reading should not be neglected. Think of men who devote six days a week to their body, which will soon pass away, but begrudge one day to the soul, which will live on and on forever. Is it too much for God to ask for one day to be devoted to the growth and training of the spiritual senses, when the other senses are kept busy the other six days?

> If your circumstances permit, engage in some definite Christian work, such as teaching in Sunday school or visiting the sick.

If your circumstances permit, engage in some definite Christian work, such as teaching in Sunday school or visiting the sick. Do all the good you can. Sin keeps no Sabbath, so good deeds shouldn't either. There is plenty of opportunity in this fallen world to perform works of mercy and religion. Make your Sabbath down here a foretaste of the eternal Sabbath that is in store for believers.

You want power in your Christian life, don't you? You want Holy Spirit power? You want the dew of heaven on your brow? You want to see men convicted and converted? I don't believe we shall ever have genuine conversions until we get straight on this law of God.

Sabbath Desecration

Men seem to think they have a right to change the holy day into a holiday. The young have more temptations to break the Sabbath than we had forty years ago. There are three great temptations: first, the trolley car, that will take you off into the country for a nickel to have a day of recreation; second, the bicycle, which is leading many Christian men to give up their Sabbath and spend the day on excursions; and third, the Sunday newspaper. (Editor's note: Obviously, we must recognize that Moody wrote in the 1800s and the means of transport and activities have only grown and multiplied.)

Twenty years ago, Christian people in Chicago would have been horrified if anyone had prophesied that all the theatres would be open every Sabbath, but that is what has come to pass. If it had been prophesied twenty years ago that Christian men would take a wheel and go off on Sunday morning and be gone all day on day trips, Christians would have been horrified and would have said it was impossible; but that is what is going on today all over the country.

The Sunday Newspaper

With regard to the Sunday newspaper, I know all the arguments that are brought in its favor – that the work on it is done during the week, that it is the Monday paper that causes Sunday work, and so on. But there are two hundred thousand newsboys selling the paper on Sunday. Would you like to have your boy be one of them? Men work to transport and distribute the papers. Would you like your Sabbath taken away from you? If not, then practice the Golden Rule and don't touch the papers.

The contents of these papers make them unfit for reading any day, much less for Sunday. Some New York dailies advertise Sunday editions of sixty pages. Many dirty pieces of scandal are in these pages, and other countries' scandals are revived and put into them. "Eight pages of fun!" – that is splendid reading for Sunday, isn't it? Even when a so-called sermon is printed, it is completely buried by the fiction and news matter. It is time that ministers went into their pulpits and preached against Sunday newspapers, if they haven't done it already. Put the man on the scale who buys and reads Sunday papers. After reading them for two or three hours, he might go and hear the best sermon in the world, but you couldn't preach anything into him. His mind is filled up with what he has read, and there is no room for thoughts of God. I believe that the archangel Gabriel himself could not make an impression on an audience that has its head full of such trash. If you bored a hole into a man's head, you could not inject any thoughts of God and heaven.

I don't believe that the publishers would allow their own children to read them. Why then should they give them to my children and to yours?

A merchant who advertises in Sunday papers is not keeping the Sabbath. It is a masterstroke of the devil to induce Christian men to do this to have business on Monday. But if a man makes money, but his sons are ruined and his home broken up, what has he gained?

Ladies buy the Sunday papers and read the advertisements of Monday bargains to see what they can buy cheap. Likewise with their religion, they are willing to have it if it doesn't cost anything. (Editor's note: Mr. Moody would be appalled to see how today most businesses stay open on Sundays.)

If Christian men and women refused to buy the newspapers and Christian merchants refused to advertise in them, they would soon die out, because that is where they get most of their support.

They tell me the Sunday paper is here to stay, and I may as well leave it alone. Never! I believe it is a great evil, and I shall fight it while I live. I never read a Sunday paper and wouldn't have one in my house. They are often sent to me, but I tear them up without reading them. I will have nothing to do with them. They do more harm to religion than any other one agency I know. Their whole influence is against keeping the Sabbath holy. They are an unnecessary evil. Can't a man read enough news on weekdays without desecrating the Sabbath? We had no Sunday papers before the war [Civil War], and we got along very well without them. They have been increasing in size and in number ever since then, and I think they have been lowering their tone ever since. If you believe that, help to fight them. Stamp them out, beginning with yourself.

Punishment or Blessing

No nation has ever prospered that has trampled the Sabbath in the dust. Show me a nation that has done this, and I will show you a nation that has the seeds of ruin and decay. I believe that Sabbath desecration will carry a nation down quicker than anything else. Adam brought marriage and the Sabbath with him out of Eden, and neither can be disregarded without suffering. When the children of Israel went into the promised land, God told them to let their land rest every seven years, and He would give them as much in six years as in seven. For four hundred and ninety years, they disregarded that law. But mark you, Nebuchadnezzar came and took them into Babylon and kept them in captivity for seventy years, and the land had its seventy Sabbaths of rest. Seven times seventy is four hundred and ninety. So they did not gain much by breaking this law. You can give God His day, or He will take it.

On the other hand, honoring the fourth commandment brings blessing. *If because of the Sabbath, you turn your foot from doing your own pleasure on My holy day, and call the Sabbath a delight, the holy day of the LORD honorable, and honor it, desisting from your own ways, from seeking your own pleasure and speaking your own word, then you will take delight in the LORD, and I will make you ride on the heights of the earth; And I will feed you with the heritage of Jacob your father, for the mouth of the LORD has spoken* (Isaiah 58:13-14).

I do not know what will become of this republic if we give up our Christian Sabbath. If Satan can break the conscience down on one point, he can break it down on all. When I was in France in 1867, I could not tell one day from the other. On Sunday, stores were open and buildings were erected as on other days. See how quickly that country declined. One hundred years ago, France and England stood abreast in the march of nations. Where do they stand today? France undertook to wipe out the Sabbath and has nearly wiped itself out, while England winds around the globe.

A Firm Stand

We have a fighting chance to save this nation, but what we need are men and women who have moral courage to stand up and say, "No, I will not touch the Sunday paper, and all the influence I have I will throw against it. I will not go away on Saturday evening if I have to travel on Sunday to get back. I will not do unnecessary work on the Sabbath. I will do all I can to keep it holy as God commanded."

But someone says, "Mr. Moody, what are you going to do? I have to work seven days a week or starve."

Then starve! Wouldn't it be a grand thing to have a martyr in the nineteenth century? "The blood of the martyrs is the seed of the church." Someone says the seed is getting very low; it has been a long time since we have had any seed. I would give something to erect a monument to such a martyr for his faithfulness to God's law. I would go around the world to attend his funeral.

We need men who will make up their minds to do what is right and stand by it if the heavens tumble on their heads. What is to become of Christian associations and Sunday schools, of churches and Christian Endeavor societies, if the Christian Sabbath is given up to recreation and made a holiday? Hasn't the time come to call a halt if men want power with God? Let men call you narrow and bigoted, but be man enough to stand by God's law, and you will have power and blessing. We need this kind of Christianity in this country. Any man can go with the crowd, but we want men who will go against the current.

Sabbath-breaker, are you ready to step on the scales?

Chapter 5

The Fifth Commandment

Honor your father and your mother, that your days may be prolonged in the land which the LORD your God gives you.
(Exodus 20:12)

We are living in dark days with this command-ment too. It seems as if the days the apostle Paul wrote about are upon us: *In the last days difficult times will come. For men will be lovers of self, lovers of money, boastful, arrogant, revilers, disobedient to parents, ungrateful, unholy, unloving, irreconcilable, malicious gossips, without self-control, brutal, haters of good* (2 Timothy 3:1-3). If Paul was alive today, could he have described the present state of affairs more accurately? There are perhaps more men in this country who are breaking the hearts of their fathers and mothers and trampling on the law of God than in any other civilized country in the world. How many sons treat their parents with contempt and make light of their requests? A young man will have the kindest care from parents; they will watch over him and care for all his wants, but some bad companion will come in and sweep him away from them in a few weeks. How many young ladies have married against their parents' wishes, left home, and made their own life bitter? I never knew one case that did not turn out badly. They invariably bring ruin upon themselves, unless they repent.

Begin in the Home

The first four commandments deal with our relationship to God. They tell us how to worship and when to worship; they forbid irreverence and disrespect in words and actions. Now God turns to our relationship with each other; isn't it significant that He deals first with family life? God is going to show us our duty to our neighbor. How does He begin? Not by telling us how kings ought to reign, or how soldiers ought to fight, or how merchants ought to conduct their business, but how boys and girls ought to behave at home.

We can see that if their home life is all right, they are almost sure to fulfill the law in regard to both God and man. Parents stand in the place of God to their children in a great many ways, until the children arrive at an age of accountability. If the children are true to their parents, it will be easier for them to be true to God. He used the human relationship as a symbol of our relationship with Him, both in creation and through grace. God is our Father in heaven. We are His offspring.

On the other hand, if they have not learned to be obedient and respectful at home, they are likely to have little respect for the law of the land. It is a matter of the heart, and the heart is prepared at home for good or bad conduct outside. The tree grows the way the twig is bent.

Honor your father and your mother. That word *honor* means more than mere obedience; a child may obey through fear. It includes love, affection, gratitude, and respect. We are told that in the East the words *father* and *mother* include those who are superiors in age, wisdom, and in civil or religious station, so when the Jews were taught to honor their father and mother, it included all who were placed over them in these relationships as well as their parents. Isn't there a crying need for that same feeling today? The lawlessness of the present time is a natural consequence of the growing absence of a feeling of respect for those in authority.

> The lawlessness of the present time is a natural consequence of the growing absence of a feeling of respect for those in authority.

Honor Thy Mother

It has been pointed out as worthy of notice that this commandment advocates honor for the mother, but in Eastern countries the woman is held in low regard to this present day. When I was in Palestine a few years ago, the prettiest girl in Jericho was sold by her father in exchange for a donkey. In many ancient nations, just as in the pagan countries today, the parents are killed off as soon as they become old and feeble. Can't we see the hand of God in this commandment, raising the woman to her rightful position of honor out of the degradation she has been dragged into by heathenism?

Honor your father and your mother, that your days may be prolonged in the land which the LORD your God gives you. I believe that we must get back to the old truths. You may make light of it and laugh at it, but remember that God has given this commandment, and you cannot set it aside. If we get back to this law, we shall have power and blessing.

Earthly Blessing or Curse

I believe it is literally true that our earthly condition depends on the way we act upon this commandment. *Honor your father and your mother (which is the first commandment with a promise), so that it may be well with you, and that you may live long on the earth* (Ephesians 6:2-3). *Honor your father and your mother, as the LORD your God has commanded you, that your days may be prolonged and that it may go well with you on the land which the LORD your God gives you* (Deuteronomy 5:16). *Cursed is he who dishonors his father or mother* (Deuteronomy 27:16). *He who curses his father or his mother, his lamp will go out in time of darkness* (Proverbs 20:20). It would be easy to multiply texts from the Bible to prove this truth. Experience teaches the same thing. A good, loving son generally

> A good, loving son generally turns out better than a disobedient son.

turns out better than a disobedient son. Obedience and respect at home prepare the way for obedience to the employer; these are joined with other virtues that lead to a prosperous career, crowned with a ripe, honored old age. Disobedience and disrespect for parents are often the first steps in the downward spiral. Many criminals have testified that this is the point where they first went astray. I have lived over sixty years, and I have learned one thing if I have learned nothing else – no man or woman who dishonors father or mother ever prospers.

Young man, young woman, how do you treat your parents? Tell me that, and I will tell you how you are going to succeed in life. When I hear a young man speaking contemptuously of his gray-haired father or mother, I say he has sunk very low indeed. When I see a young man as polite as any gentleman can be when he is out in society, but snaps at his mother and speaks unkindly to his father, I would not care at all for his religion. If there is any man or woman on earth who should be treated with kindness and tenderness, it is that loving mother or that loving father. If they cannot have your respect through life, what reward are they to have for all their care and anxiety? Think how they loved you and provided for you in your early days.

A Mother's Love

Let your mind go back to a time when you were ill. Did your mother neglect you? When a neighbor came in and said, "Now, mother, you go and lie down; you have been up for a week; I will take your place for a night," did she do it? No. And if her poor, worn body forced her at last to rest, she lay watching; if she heard your voice, she was at your side immediately, anticipating all your needs and wiping the perspiration away from your brow. If you wanted water, she quickly got it! She would gladly have taken the disease into her own body to save you. Her love for you would have driven her to any lengths. No matter how deep into vice and misery you have sunk, no matter how immoral you have grown, she has not turned you out of her heart. Perhaps she loves you all the more because you are wayward, for she would draw you back by the bands of a love that never dies.

Ingratitude of Children

When I was in England, I read of a man who professed to be a Christian and was brought before the magistrate for not supporting his elderly father. He had let him go to the poorhouse. My friends, I'd rather be content with a crust of bread and a drink of water than let my father or mother go to the poorhouse. The idea of a professing Christian doing such a thing! God have mercy on such a godless Christianity as that! It is a withered-up thing, and the breath of heaven will drive it away. Don't profess to love God and do a thing like that.

A friend of mine told me of a poor man who had sent his son to school in the city. One day the father was hauling some wood into the city, perhaps to pay his boy's bills. The young man was walking down the street with two of his school friends, all dressed in high-class fashion. His father saw him and was so glad to see him that he left his wood and went to the sidewalk to speak to him. But the boy was ashamed of his father, who wore his old working clothes, and spurned him and said, "I don't know you."

Will such a young man ever amount to anything? Never!

I remember a very promising young man whom I had in the Sunday school in Chicago. His father was a confirmed drunkard, and his mother took in washing to pay for education for their four children. This young man was her eldest son, and I thought that he was going to redeem the whole family. But one day something happened that lowered my opinion of him.

The boy was in high school and was a very bright scholar. One day he stood with his mother at the cottage door of a poorhouse. She could not pay for their schooling, and feed and clothe her children, and rent a good house all out of her earnings. While they were talking, a young man from the high school came up the street, and this boy walked away from his mother. The next day the young man said, "Who was that I saw you talking to yesterday?"

"Oh, that was my washerwoman."

I said, "Poor fellow! He will never amount to anything."

That was many years ago. I have kept my eye on him. He has gone down, down, down, and now he is just a miserable wreck. Of course he went down, because he was ashamed of his mother who loved him and labored for him and bore so much hardship for him! I cannot tell you the contempt I had for that one act.

A Brighter Picture

Some years ago I heard of a poor woman who sent her boy to school and college. When he was about to graduate, he invited his mother to come, but she wrote back that she could not because her only skirt had already been resewn once. She was so shabby that she was afraid he would be ashamed of her. He wrote back that he didn't care how she was dressed and urged her so strongly that she went. He met her at the station and took her to a nice place to stay. The day came for his graduation, and he walked down the broad aisle with that poor mother dressed very shabbily and put her into one of the best seats in the house. To her great surprise, he was the valedictorian of the class. He won a prize, and when it was given to him, he stepped down before the whole audience, kissed his mother, and said, "Here, mother, here is the prize. It is yours. I would not have had it if it had not been for you."

Thank God for such a man!

The one glimpse the Bible gives us of thirty out of the thirty-three years of Christ's life on earth shows that He did not come to destroy this fifth commandment. The secret of all those silent years is embodied in that verse in Luke's gospel: *And He went down with them and came to Nazareth, and He continued in subjection to them* (Luke 2:51). Didn't He set an example of true filial love and care when in the midst of the agonies of the cross He made provision for His mother? Didn't He condemn the miserable evasions of this law by the Pharisees of His own day when He said, *You hypocrites, rightly did Isaiah prophesy of you: This people honors me with their lips, but their heart is far away from me. But in vain do they worship me, teaching as doctrines the precepts of men* (Matthew 15:7-9).

> *Neglecting the commandment of God, you hold to the tradition of men . . . For Moses said, 'Honour your father and your mother', and, 'He who speaks evil of father or mother, is to be put to death'. But you say, 'If a man says to his father or his mother, whatever I have that would help you is Corban (that is to say, given to God),' you no longer permit him to do anything for his father or his mother; thus invalidating the word of God by your tradition which you have handed down.* (Mark 7:8, 10-13)

I have read of one pagan custom in China, which would be good for us in this so-called Christian country. On every New Year's Day morning, each man and boy, from the emperor to the lowest peasant, pays a visit to his mother and carries a present to her, varying in value according to his station in life. He thanks her for all she has done for him and asks for her continued favor for another year. Abraham Lincoln used to say, "All I have I owe to my mother."

> I would rather die a hundred deaths than have my children grow up to treat me with scorn and contempt.

I would rather die a hundred deaths than have my children grow up to treat me with scorn and contempt. I would rather have them honor me a thousand times over than have the world honor me. I would rather have their esteem and favor than the esteem of the whole world. And any man who seeks the honor and esteem of the world but doesn't treat his parents well is sure to be disappointed.

An Exhortation

Young man, if your parents are still living, treat them with kindness. Do all you can to make their declining years sweet and happy. Bear in mind that this is the only commandment that you may not always be able to obey. As long as you live, you will be able to serve God, to keep the Sabbath, and to obey all the other commandments; but the day comes to most men when father and mother die. What bitter feelings you will have when the opportunity to bless them is gone, if you fail to show them the respect and love that is their due! How long has it been since you wrote to your mother? Perhaps you have not written home for months, or maybe for years. How often I get letters from mothers urging me to try to influence their sons!

Which would you rather be – a Joseph or an Absalom? Joseph wasn't satisfied until he had brought his old father down to Egypt. Next to Pharaoh he was the greatest man in Egypt; he was arrayed in the finest garments; he had Pharaoh's ring on his hand and a gold chain about his neck. They cried before him, "Bow the knee!" Yet when he heard Jacob was coming, he hurried out to meet him. He wasn't ashamed of the old man in his shepherd's clothes.

What a contrast we see in Absalom. That young

man broke his father's heart by his rebellion, and the Jews are said to throw a stone at Absalom's pillar to this day, whenever they pass it, as a token of their horror at Absalom's irreverent conduct.

Now, are you ready to be weighed? If you have been dishonoring your father and mother, step on the scales and see how quickly you will be found wanting. I don't know any man who is much lighter than one who treats his parents with contempt. Do you disobey them just as much as you dare? Do you try to deceive them? Do you call them old-fashioned and sneer at their advice? How do you treat that faithful father and praying mother?

You may be a professing Christian, but I wouldn't give much for your religion unless it gets into your life and teaches you how to live. I wouldn't care for a religion that doesn't begin at home and regulates your conduct toward your parents.

Chapter 6

The Sixth Commandment

You shall not murder. (Exodus 20:13)

I used to say, "What is the use of discussing a law like this in an audience where there probably isn't a man who ever thought of, or ever will, commit murder?" But as one gets older, he sees many murders that are not outright killing. I don't need to kill a person to be a murderer. If I get so angry that I wish a man dead, I am a murderer in God's sight. God looks at the heart and says he who hates his brother is a murderer.

First, let's see what this commandment does not mean. It does not forbid the killing of animals for food and for other reasons. Millions of rams, lambs, and turtledoves must have been killed every year for sacrifices under the Mosaic system. Christ Himself ate of the Passover lamb, and we are told of cases where He ate fish and provided it for His disciples and the people to eat.

It does not forbid the killing of burglars in self-defense. After giving the Ten Commandments, God laid down the ordinance that *if the thief is caught while breaking in and is struck so that he dies, there will be no bloodguiltiness on his account* (Exodus 22:2). Didn't Christ justify this idea of self-defense when He said, *if the head of the house had known at what time of the night the thief was coming, he would have been on the alert and would not have allowed his house to be broken into* (Matthew 24:43)?

Scripture does not forbid capital punishment. God Himself set the death penalty upon violations of each of the first seven commandments as well as for other crimes. God said to Noah after the deluge, *Whoever sheds man's blood, by man his blood shall be shed*, and the reason given is just as true today as it was then: *for in the image of God He made man* (Genesis 9:6).

What it does forbid is the malicious, intentional taking of human life under wrong motives and circumstances. Man is made in God's image. He is built for eternity. He is more than a mere animal. His life should therefore be held sacred. Once taken, it can never be restored. In heathen lands, human life is no more sacred than the life of animals; even in Christian lands, there are heartless and selfish men who do not value life; but God has invested life with a high value. An infidel philosopher of the eighteenth century said, "But the life of a man is of no greater importance to the universe than that of an oyster."[8] "Where then is

---

8   David Hume, *Essays, Moral, Political, and Literary, Part III, Essay IX, Section 9, www.econlib.org/library/LFBooks/ Hume/hmMPL48.html.*

the crime," he asked, "of turning a few ounces of blood from their natural chanels?"[9] Such language needs no answer.

The Value of a Man

Let me give you a passage from H. L. Hastings:

> A friend of mine visited the Fiji Islands in 1844, and what do you suppose an infidel was worth there at that time? You could buy an infidel for a musket, or for $7.00 in money. And after you had bought your man, you could do with him what you pleased. You could feed him, starve him, work him, whip him, or eat him. They generally ate them. But if you should go there today, you could not buy a man for $7,000,000. No men are for sale there now. What has brought about the change? What has brought about this difference in the market price of humanity? Twelve hundred Christian chapels, scattered over the islands, tell the story.

The people had learned to read that Book which says, *knowing that you were not redeemed with perishable things like silver or gold from your futile way of life inherited from your forefathers, but with precious blood, as of a lamb unblemished and spotless, the blood of Christ* (1 Peter 1:18-19), and since they learned that lesson, no man is for sale there.

Men tell me that the world is getting so much better.

---

9   David Hume, *Essays, Moral, Political, and Literary, Part III, Essay IX, Section 12.*

We talk of our American civilization. We forget the alarming increase of crime in our midst. Some reports say there is no civilized country on the globe where murder is so frequently committed and so seldom punished.

Suicide

Another kind of murder is increasing at an appalling rate among us – suicide. Some infidels of all ages have advocated it as a justifiable means of release from trial and difficulty, but thinking men, as far back as Aristotle, have generally condemned it as cowardly and unjustifiable under any conditions. No man has a right to take his own life from such motives any more than he has the right to take the life of another.

> No man has a right to take his own life.

The Jewish race, the people of God, always counted length of days as a blessing. The Bible does not mention one single instance of a good man committing suicide. The four thousand years of Old Testament history record only four suicides and only one suicide is recorded in the New Testament. King Saul of Israel, Saul's armor-bearer, Ahithophel, Zimri, and Judas Iscariot are the five cases. Look at the references in the Bible to see what kind of men they were.

Other Kinds of Murder

But I want to speak of other types of murderers that are numerous in this country, although they are not classified as murderers. The man who is the cause of the death of another through criminal carelessness is guilty. The man who sells diseased meat, the saloonkeeper whose drink has maddened the brain of a criminal, those who contaminate food, and the employer who jeopardizes the lives of employees and others by unsafe surroundings and conditions in harmful occupations are all guilty of blood where life is lost as a consequence.

When I was in England in 1892, I met a gentleman who claimed England was ahead of us in the respect they had for the law. "We hang our murderers," he said, "but there isn't one out of twenty in your country that is hung."

I said, "You are greatly mistaken, for they walk about these two countries unhung."

"What do you mean?"

"I will tell you what I mean," I said. "The man that comes into my house and runs a dagger into my heart for my money is a prince compared with a son that takes five years to kill me and my beloved wife. A young man who comes home drunk night after night and curses his mother's gray hairs and kills her by inches is the blackest kind of a murderer."

That kind of thing is going on constantly all around us. One young man at college, an only son, whose mother wrote to him disapproving of his gambling and drinking habits, took the letters out of the post office; when he saw that they were from her, he tore them up without reading them.

She said, "I thought I would die when I found I had lost my influence on that son."

If a boy kills his mother by his conduct, you can't

call it anything else than *murder*, and he is as truly guilty of breaking this sixth commandment as if he drove a dagger through her heart. If all young men in this country who are killing their parents and their wives by inches should be hung this next week, there would be a great many funerals.

How are you treating your parents? Come, are you killing them? This sixth commandment follows very naturally after the fifth: *Honor your father and your mother.* Don't put any thorns in their pillows and make their last days miserable. Bear in mind that the commandment refers not only to shooting a man down in cold blood, but also that the worst murderer is the one who goes on, month after month, year after year, until he has crowded the life out of a sainted mother and put a godly father in the grave.

The Words of Christ

Let us look once again at the Sermon on the Mount, that men think so much of, and see what Christ had to say. *You have heard that the ancients were told, 'You shall not commit murder', and 'Whoever commits murder shall be liable to the court.' But I say to you that everyone who is angry with his brother shall be guilty before the court; and whoever says to his brother, 'You good-for-nothing,' shall be guilty before the supreme court; and whoever says, 'You fool,' shall be guilty enough to go into the fiery hell* (Matthew 5:21-22).

"Three degrees of murderous guilt," it has been said, "all of which can be manifested without a blow being struck: secret anger, the spiteful jeer, and the open, unrestrained outburst of violent, abusive speech."

Again, what does John say? *Everyone who hates his brother is a murderer; and you know that no murderer has eternal life abiding in him* (1 John 3:15).

Did you ever in your heart wish a man dead? That was murder. Did you ever get so angry that you wished someone harm? Then you are guilty. I may be addressing someone who is cultivating an unforgiving spirit. That is the spirit of the murderer and needs to be rooted out of your heart.

We can only read man's actions – what he has done. God looks down into the heart. That is the birthplace and home of the evil desires and intentions that lead to the transgression of all God's laws.

Listen once more to the words of Jesus: *For from within, out of the heart of men, proceed the evil thoughts, fornications, thefts, murders, adulteries, deeds of coveting and wickedness, as well as deceit, sensuality, envy, slander, pride and foolishness* (Mark 7:21-22).

May God purge our hearts of these evil things, if we are harboring them! Ah, if many of us were weighed now, we should find Belshazzar's doom written against us – *Tekel wanting*!

Chapter 7

The Seventh Commandment

You shall not commit adultery.
(Exodus 20:14)

An English army officer in India who had been living an impure life went around one evening to argue religion with the chaplain. During their talk, the officer said, "Religion is all very well, but you must admit that there are difficulties – with the miracles, for instance."

The chaplain knew the man and his embarrassing sin and quietly looked him in the face and answered, "Yes, there are some things in the Bible not very plain, I admit, but the seventh commandment is very plain."

Plain Speaking

I wish I could pass over this commandment, but I feel that the time has come to cry aloud and not spare. Plain speaking about it is not very fashionable today.

"Teachers of religion have by common consent banished from their public teaching all advice, warning, or allusion in regard to love between the sexes," says Dr. Stalker. These themes are left to poets and novelists to handle. In an autobiography recently published in England, the writer attributed no small share of the follies and vices of his earlier years to his never having heard a plain, outspoken sermon on this seventh commandment.

But though men are inclined to pass it by, God is not silent or indifferent about adultery. When I hear anyone make light of adultery and licentiousness, I take the Bible and see how God has let His curse and wrath come down upon it.

> *You shall not commit adultery.*
> (Exodus 20:14)

> *For that would be a lustful crime; Moreover, it would be an iniquity punishable by judges. For it would be fire that consumes to Abaddon, and would uproot all my increase.*
> (Job 31:11-12)

> *For on account of a harlot one is reduced to a loaf of bread, and an adulteress hunts for the precious life. Can a man take fire in his bosom and his clothes not be burned? Or can a man walk on hot coals and his feet not be scorched? So is the one who goes in to his neighbor's wife; Whoever touches her will not go unpunished. The one who*

*commits adultery with a woman is lack-
ing sense; He who would destroy himself
does it. Wounds and disgrace he will find,
and his reproach will not be blotted out.*
(Proverbs 6:26-29, 32-33)

*Or do you not know that the unrighteous
will not inherit the kingdom of God? Do
not be deceived; neither fornicators, nor
idolaters, nor adulterers, nor effeminate,
nor homosexuals, nor thieves, nor the covetous, nor drunkards, nor revilers, nor
swindlers, will inherit the kingdom of God.*
(1 Corinthians 6:9-10)

*But immorality or any impurity or greed
must not even be named among you, as is
proper among saints; and there must be no
filthiness and silly talk, or coarse jesting,
which are not fitting, but rather giving of
thanks. For this you know with certainty, that
no immoral or impure person or covetous
man, who is an idolater, has an inheritance
in the kingdom of Christ and God. Let no one
deceive you with empty words, for because of
these things the wrath of God comes upon the
sons of disobedience. Therefore do not be par-
takers with them.* (Ephesians 5:3-7)

*Immoral persons . . ., their part will be in
the lake that burns with fire and brimstone,*

> *which is the second death. . . . Outside are . . .*
> *the immoral persons.* (Revelation 21:8; 22:15)

These are a few of the threatenings and warnings contained in the Book, from the beginning to its closing chapter. It speaks plainly and without compromise.

Marriage and the Home

This commandment is God's bulwark around marriage and the home. Marriage is one of the institutions that existed in Eden; it is older than the fall. It is the most sacred relationship that can exist between human beings, taking precedence even over the relationship of the parent and child. Someone has pointed out that as in the beginning God created one man and one woman, this is the true order for all ages. When family ties are disregarded and dishonored, the results are always fatal. The home existed before the church, and unless the home is kept pure and undefiled, family religion cannot exist, and the church is in danger. Adultery and licentiousness have swept nation after nation out of existence. Didn't it bring fire and brimstone from heaven upon Sodom and Gomorrah? What carried Rome into ruin? The obscene frescoes and statues at Pompeii and Naples tell the tale. Where there is no sacredness around the home, population dwindles, family virtues disappear, children are corrupt from their birth, and seeds of decay are planted. In 1895 there were twenty-five thousand divorces in this country.[10]

---

10 In America in 2016, there is one divorce approximately every 36 seconds. That's nearly 2,400 divorces per day, 16,800 per week, and 876,000 per year. McKinley Irvin Family Law: *www.mckinleyirvin.com/Family-Law-Blog/ 2012/October/32-Shocking-Divorce-Statistics.aspx.*

I was on an upscale street of a prominent city some time ago, where every family except two had either a son or a daughter that had been divorced. Divorce and debauchery go hand in hand. We are not gaining much in turning away from this old law, are we?

The Devil's Counterfeit

Lust is the devil's counterfeit of love. There is nothing more beautiful on earth than a pure love, and there is nothing so destructive as lust. I do not know of a quicker, shorter way down to hell than by adultery and the kindred sins condemned by this commandment. The Bible

> Lust is the devil's counterfeit of love.

says that *with the heart a person believes, resulting in righteousness,* but *harlotry, wine and new wine take away the understanding* (Romans 10:10; Hosea 4:11). Lust will drive all natural affection out of a man's heart. For the sake of some vile prostitute, he will trample on the feelings and entreaties of a saintly and beautiful wife.

Young man, are you leading an impure life? Suppose God's scales should drop down before you; what would you do? Are you fit for the kingdom of heaven? You know very well that you are not. You loathe yourself. When you observe the pure life or your wife or mother, you say, "What a vile wretch I am! Unrestrained sensuality is bringing me down to an untimely and dishonored grave."

May God show us what a fearful sin this is! The idea of making light of it! I do not know of any sin that will make a man descend to ruin more quickly. I am appalled when I think of what is going on in the world – so many young men living impure lives and talking about the virtue of women as if it didn't mean anything. This sin is rushing upon us like a flood at the present day. In every city there is an army of prostitutes. Young men by the hundreds are being utterly ruined by this accursed sin.

The Prodigal Daughter

I think that the most infernal thing the sun shines on in America is the way a woman is treated after she has been ruined by a man, often under fair promises of marriage. When the Prodigal Son came home, he had the best robe and the fatted calf, but what does the prodigal daughter get? Although she may have been more sinned against than sinning, she is cast out and ostracized by society. She is condemned to an almost hopeless life of degradation and shame, sinking into a loathsome grave, unless she hurries her doom by suicide. But the wretch who has ruined her in body and soul holds his head as high as ever, and society attaches no stain to him. If he had failed to pay his gambling debts or was detected cheating at cards, he would promptly be dropped by society; but he may boast of his impure life, and his companions will think nothing of it. Parents who would not allow their daughters to become acquainted with a man who is rude in manners sometimes do not hesitate to accept the society of men who are known to be impure.

Talk about stealing – a man who steals the virtue of a woman is the meanest thief that ever was on the face of the earth! One who goes into your house and steals your money is a prince compared with a vile womanizer who takes the virtue of your sister or steals the affection of your wife and robs you of her; no sneak-thief that ever walked the earth is as mean as he is. How men pass laws to protect their property, but when that which is much nearer and dearer to them is taken, it is made light of! If a man pushed a young lady into the river and she drowned, the law would arrest him, and he would be tried for murder. But if he wins her affection and ruins her and then casts her off, isn't he worse than a murderer? There are some sins that are worse than murder, and that is one of them. If someone treated your wife or sister like that, you would want to shoot him. Why do you not respect all women as you do your mother and sister? "What law of justice forgives the obscene bird of prey, while it kicks out of its path the soiled and bleeding dove?"[11]

God's Coming Judgment

God has appointed a day when this matter will be set right. *Do not be deceived, God is not mocked; for whatever a man sows, this he will also reap* (Galatians 6:7). He will render to every man according to his deeds. You may walk down the aisle of the church and take your seat, thinking that no one knows of your sin. But God is on the throne, and He will surely bring you to judgment. Do you believe that God will allow this infernal thing to go on – women bearing all the blame

---

11   Frederic William Farrar, *The Voice from Sinai: The Eternal Bases of the Moral Law* (New York: Thomas Whittaker, 1892), 220.

while guilty men go unpunished? God has appointed a day when He will judge this world in righteousness, and the day is fast approaching.

If you are guilty of this sin, do not let the day pass until you repent. If you are living in some secret sin or fostering impure thoughts, make up your mind that by the grace of God you will be delivered. I don't believe a man who is guilty of this sin is ever going to see the kingdom of God unless he repents and does all he can to make restitution.

An Evil Harvest

Even in this life, adultery and uncleanness have awful consequences, both physical and mental. The pleasure and excitement that lead so many astray at the beginning soon pass away, and only the evil remains. Vice carries a sting in its tail like the scorpion. The body is sinned against, and the body eventually suffers. *Every other sin that a man commits is outside the body, but the immoral man sins against his own body*, said Paul (1 Corinthians 6:18). Nature itself punishes with nameless diseases, and the man goes down to the grave rotten, leaving the effects of his sin to corrupt his descendants. There are nations whose manhood has been destroyed by this awful scourge.

It drags a man lower than the beasts. It stains the memory. I believe that memory is the worm that never dies, and the memory is never cleansed of obscene stories and unclean acts. Even if a man repents and reforms, he often has to fight the past.

Lust led David to commit murder and called down upon him the wrath of God; if he had not repented, he would have lost heaven (2 Samuel 11:14-17; 12:9-15). I believe that if Joseph had responded to the enticement of Potiphar's wife, his light would have gone out in darkness (Genesis 39:7-12).

Adultery ends in one of two ways: either in remorse and shame because of the realization of the loss of purity, or in hardness of heart, brutalizing to the finer senses, which is a more dreadful condition.

We hear much about passions today. That sin advertises itself; it shows its marks upon faces and in conduct, but hides itself in the shadow of the night. A man who dabbles with this evil continues step by step until his character is crushed, his reputation ruined, his health gone, and his life made as dark as hell. May God wake the nation up to see how this awful sin is spreading!

Will anyone deny that the house of the strange woman *is the way to Sheol* [hell], *descending to the chambers of death*, as the Bible says (Proverbs 7:27)? Are there not men whose characters have been utterly ruined for this life through this accursed sin? Are there not wives who would rather sink into their graves than live? Many a man went with a pure woman to the altar a few years ago and promised to love and cherish her. Now he has given his affections to some vile call girl and brought ruin on his wife and children!

Are You Guilty?

Young man, young woman, are you guilty in thought? Bear in mind what Christ said: *You have heard that it was said, 'You shall not commit adultery'; but I say to you that everyone who looks at a woman with lust for her has already committed adultery with her in his heart* (Matthew 5:27-28). How many would repent, but they are tied hand and foot, and some prostitute, whose feet are fastened in hell, clings to him and says, "If you give me up, I will expose you!" Can you step on the scales and take the fallen woman with you?

If you are guilty of this awful sin, run for your life. Hear God's voice while there is still time. Confess your sin to Him. Ask Him to break the chains that bind you. Ask Him to give you victory over your passions. If your right eye offends, pluck it out. If your right hand offends, cut it off. Shake yourself like Samson and say, "By the grace of God I will not go down to an adulterer's grave."

There is hope for you, adulterer. There is hope for you, adulteress. God will not turn you away if you repent. No matter how low down in vice and misery you may have sunk, you may be washed, you may be sanctified, and you may be justified in the name of the Lord Jesus and by the Spirit of our God. Remember what Christ said to that woman who was a sinner: *Your sins have been forgiven. Your faith has saved you; go in peace*, and to that woman that was taken in adultery, *Go. From now on sin no more* (Luke 7:48, 50; John 8:11).

Chapter 8

The Eighth Commandment

You shall not steal. (Exodus 20:15)

During the time of slavery, a slave was preaching with great power. His master heard about it, sent for him, and said, "I understand you are preaching?"

"Yes," said the slave.

"Well, now," said the master, "I will give you all the time you need, and I want you to prepare a sermon on the Ten Commandments and stress particularly stealing, because there is a great deal of stealing on the plantation."

The slave's countenance fell at once. He said he didn't want to do that because there wasn't the warmth in that subject that there was in others.

I have noticed that people are satisfied when you preach about the sins of the patriarchs, but they don't like it when you touch on the sins of today. That hits too close to home. But we need to have these old doctrines stated over and over again in our churches. Perhaps it is not necessary to speak here about the grosser violations of this eighth commandment, because the law of the land looks after those; but a man or woman can steal without cracking safes and picking pockets. Many people shrink from taking what belongs to another person but think nothing of stealing from the government or from large public corporations.

If you steal from a rich man, it is as much a sin as stealing from a poor man.

If you steal from a rich man, it is as much a sin as stealing from a poor man. If you lie about the value of things you buy, aren't you trying to cheat the customer? *"Bad, bad," says the buyer, but when he goes his way, then he boasts* (Proverbs 20:14).

On the other hand, many people who would not steal themselves, hold stock in companies that make dishonest profits, but *do not be bound together with unbelievers; for what partnership have righteousness and lawlessness, or what fellowship has light with darkness?* (2 Corinthians 6:14).

A young man in our Bible Institute in Chicago got on the cable car, and before the conductor came around to take the fare, they reached the Institute, and he jumped off without paying his fare. In thinking over that act, he said, "That was just not right. I had my ride and I ought to pay the fare."

He remembered the face of the conductor, found him, and paid him the five cents.

"Well," the conductor said, "you are a fool not to keep it."

"No," the young man said, "I am not. I got the ride, and I ought to have paid for it."

"But it was my business to collect it."

"No, it was my business to hand it to you."

The conductor said, "I think you must belong to that Bible Institute."

I have heard few things said of the Institute that pleased me as much as that one thing. Not long after that, the conductor came to the Institute and asked the student to come to see him. A Bible study was started in his house, and not only he but also a number of others who came were converted as a result of that one act.

You can seldom pick up a newspaper without reading of some cashier of a bank who stole, or some large swindling operation that ruined scores of people, or some breach of trust or fraudulent failure in business. These things are going on all over the land.

I wish that we could have all gambling swept away, because it leads to stealing. If Christian men take the right stand, they can check it and break it up in a great many places.

Where the Stream Starts

The stream generally starts at home and in the school. Parents are woefully lax in their condemnation and punishment of stealing. The child might begin by taking candy. The mother makes light of it at first, and the child's conscience is violated without any sense of wrong. Soon it is not an easy matter to change the habit, because it grows and multiplies with every new commission.

The value of the thing that is stolen has nothing to do with the guilt of the act. Two people were once arguing on this point, and one said, "Well, you don't say that the theft of a pin and of a dollar are the same to God, do you?"

"When you tell me the difference between the value of a pin and of a dollar to God," said the other, "I will answer your question."

The value or amount is not what is to be considered, but whether the act is right or wrong. Partial obedience is not enough; obedience must be complete. The little indulgences, the small transgressions are what drive religion out of the soul. They lay the foundation for the grosser sins. If you give way to little temptations, you will not be able to resist when great temptations come to you.

God's Weights

Do you extort money or information from another? Are you ready to step on the scales? What will you do with this condemnation of God: *In you they have taken bribes to shed blood; you have taken interest and profits, and you have injured your neighbors for gain by oppression, and you have forgotten Me, declares the Lord GOD* (Ezekiel 22:12)?

Employer, are you guilty of over-working your employees? Have you defrauded the worker of his wages? Have you paid starvation wages? *You shall not oppress a hired servant who is poor and needy, whether he is one of your countrymen or one of your aliens who is in your land in your towns* (Deuteronomy 24:14). *What do you mean by crushing My people and grinding the face of the poor? Declares the Lord GOD of hosts* (Isaiah 3:15). *Behold, the pay of the laborers who mowed your fields, and which has been withheld by you, cries out against you; and the outcry of those who did the harvesting has reached the ears of the Lord of Sabaoth* (James 5:4).

And you, the one who is employed, have you been honest with your employer? Have you robbed him by wasting your time when he was not looking? If God should summon you into His presence now, what would you say?

Let the merchant step on the scales. How will you fare when weighed against the law of God? Are you guilty of cheating in your sales? Do you substitute inferior grades of goods? Are your advertisements deceptive? Are your cheap prices made possible by defrauding your customers in quantity or in quality? Do you teach your clerks to put wrong labels on items and then sell them for more money? Do you tell them to say that the goods are all wool when you know they are half cotton? Do you give short weight or measure? See what God says in His Word: *Can I justify wicked scales and a bag of deceptive weights?* (Micah 6:11). *You shall not have in your bag differing weights, a large and a small. You shall not have in your house differing measures, a large and a small. You shall have a full and just weight; you shall have a full and just measure, that your days may be prolonged in the land which the LORD your God gives you* (Deuteronomy 25:13-15). *You shall do no wrong in judgment, in measurement of weight, or capacity. You shall have just balances, just weights, a just ephah, and a just hin* (Leviticus 19:35-36). Are you like those who said, *When will the new moon be over, so that we may sell grain, and the sabbath, that we may open the wheat market, to make the bushel smaller and the shekel bigger, and to cheat with dishonest scales, so as to buy the helpless for money and the needy for a pair of sandals, and that we may sell the refuse of the wheat* (Amos 8:5-6)?

"Show me a people whose trade is dishonest," said Fronde, "and I will show you a people whose religion is a sham."[12] Unless your religion can keep you honest in your business, it isn't worth much; it isn't the right kind. God is a God of righteousness, and no true follower of His can swerve one inch to the right or left without disobeying Him.

Burden of Stolen Goods

I heard about a boy who stole a cannonball from a navy yard. He watched for his opportunity, sneaked into the yard, and secured it. But when he had it, he didn't know what to do with it. It was heavy and too large to conceal in his pocket, so he had to put it under his hat. When he got home with it, he didn't dare show it to his parents, because it would have led to his detection. In later years, he said it was the last thing he ever stole.

Another story is told that one of Queen Victoria's diamonds valued at $600,000 was stolen from the window of a jeweler who had been hired to set it. A few months later, a destitute man died a miserable death in a poor

---

12   Fronde, *Indiana State Sentinel, Volume 27, No. 66* (November 20, 1878).

rooming house. In his pocket was the diamond and a letter telling how he did not dare to sell it because it would lead to his discovery and imprisonment. It never brought him anything but anxiety and pain.

Everything you steal is a curse to you in that way. The sin overreaches itself. A man who takes money that does not belong to him never gets any lasting comfort. He has no real pleasure, for he has a guilty conscience. He cannot look an honest man in the face. He loses peace of mind here and all hope of heaven hereafter. *As a partridge that hatches eggs which it has not laid, so is he who makes a fortune, but unjustly; In the midst of his days it will forsake him, and in the end he will be a fool* (Jeremiah 17:11). [Let] *no man transgress and defraud his brother in the matter because the Lord is the avenger in all these things* (1 Thessalonians 4:6).

I may be speaking to some clerk who perhaps took five cents out of his employer's drawer to buy a cigar today, or perhaps he took ten cents to get a shave and thinks he will put it back tomorrow; no one will ever know it. If you have taken a cent, you are a thief. Do you ever think how those little episodes of stealing may bring you to ruin? Let your employer find out. If he doesn't take you to court, he will fire you. Your future hopes will be ruined, and it will be hard work to start over. Whatever condition you are in, do not take a cent that does not belong to you. Rather than steal, go up to heaven in poverty – go up to heaven from the poorhouse. Be honest, rather than go through the world in a gilded chariot of stolen riches.

Restitution

If you have ever taken money dishonestly, you don't need to pray to God to forgive you and fill you with the Holy Spirit until you make restitution. If you don't have the money now to pay it back, will yourself to do it, and God accepts the willing mind.

Many men are kept in darkness and unrest because they fail to obey God on this point. If the plough has gone deep, if the repentance is true, it will bring forth fruit. What use is there in my coming to God until I am willing to make it good if I have done any man wrong or have taken anything from him falsely? Zacchaeus was a good example of this when he said, *Behold, Lord, half of my possessions I will give to the poor, and if I have defrauded anyone of anything, I will give back four times as much* (Luke 19:8). *If a wicked man restores a pledge, pays back what he has taken by robbery, walks by the statutes which ensure life without committing iniquity, he shall surely live; he shall not die. None of his sins that he has committed will be remembered against him* (Ezekiel 33:15-16). Confession and restitution are the steps that lead to forgiveness. Until you tread those steps, you may expect your conscience to be troubled, and your sin to haunt you.

I was preaching in British Columbia some years ago,

Confession and restitution are the steps that lead to forgiveness.

and a young man came to me and wanted to become a Christian. He had been smuggling opium into the States.

"Well, my friend," I said, "I don't think there is any chance for you to become a Christian until you make restitution."

He said, "If I attempt to do that, I will fall into the clutches of the law, and I will go to the penitentiary."

"Well," I replied, "you had better do that than go to the judgment seat of God with that sin on your soul and have eternal punishment. The Lord will be very merciful if you set your face to do right."

He went away sorrowful but came back the next day and said, "I have a young wife and child, and all the furniture in my house I bought with money I got in this dishonest way. If I become a Christian, that furniture will have to go, and my wife will know it."

"Better let your wife know it, and better let your home and furniture go."

"Would you come and see my wife?" he asked. "I don't know what she will say."

I went to see her, and when I told her, the tears trickled down her cheeks, and she said, "Mr. Moody, I will gladly give everything if my husband can become a true Christian."

She took out her pocketbook and handed over her last penny. He had a piece of land in the United States, which he deeded over to the government. I do not know in all my years of any living man who has had a better testimony for Jesus Christ than that man. He had been dishonest, but when the truth came to him that he must make it right before God would help him, he made it right, and then God used him wonderfully.

No amount of weeping over sin and saying that you feel sorry is going to help unless you are willing to confess and make restitution.

Chapter 9

The Ninth Commandment

You shall not bear false witness against your neighbor. (Exodus 20:16)

Two out of the Ten Commandments deal with sins that find expression by the tongue: the third commandment, which forbids taking God's name in vain, and the ninth commandment, which forbids false witness against our neighbor. This two-fold prohibition ought to impress us as a solemn warning, especially as we find that the pages of Scripture are full of condemnation of sins of the tongue. The Psalms, Proverbs, and the epistle of James deal largely with the subject.

Truth Is Necessary
Organized society of a degree higher than that of the herding of animals and flocking of birds depends on the power of speech; without it, society would be impossible. Language is an essential element in the social fabric.

To fulfill its purpose, it must be trustworthy. Words must command confidence. Anything that undermines the truth takes the mortar out of the building, which results in ruin. Paul said, *Therefore, laying aside falsehood, speak truth each one of you with his neighbor, for we are members of one another* (Ephesians 4:25). Note the reason given – *we are members of one another.* All community, all union, and all fellowship would be shattered if a man did not know whether to believe his neighbor or not.

The transgressions of this commandment are frequent and varied in form. Men and women of all ages need to guard against them. They include some of the most troublesome sins. David said in his haste, *All men are liars* (Psalm 116:11). Someone has remarked that if David was living today, he might say it without haste and not be very far from the truth.

Perjury

The bearing of false witness is forbidden, but this must not be limited to testimony given in the law court or under oath. Isn't it a condemnation that men have to be put under oath in order to make sure of their speaking the truth? As a legal offense, perjury, which is the bearing of false witness when under oath, is one of the most serious crimes that can be committed. Nearly every civilized nation rewards it with heavy punishment. Unless promptly checked, it would shake the very foundations of justice.

Lying, the uttering of falsehood, and slander, the spreading of false reports tending to destroy the reputation of another, are two of the most common violations of this commandment.

Lying

We tend to divide lies into white lies and black lies, society lies and business lies. The Word of God knows no such lowering of the standard. A lie is a lie, no matter what the circumstances are under which it is uttered or by whom. I have heard that in the Far East they sew the mouth shut of a confirmed liar. I am afraid if that were the custom in America, many would suffer with a closed

Tell one lie and you are forced to tell others to back it up.

mouth. Parents should begin with their children while they are young and teach them to be strictly truthful at all times. There is a proverb: "A lie has no legs." It requires other lies to support it. Tell one lie and you are forced to tell others to back it up.

Slander

You don't like to have anyone bear false witness against you or ruin your character or reputation; then why should you do it to others? How public men are slandered in this country! None escape, whether good or bad. Judgment is passed upon them, their family, and their character by the press and by individuals who know little or nothing about them. If one-tenth of what is said and written about our public men were true, half of them should be in prison. Slander has been called "tongue murder." Slanderers are compared to flies that always settle on sores but do not touch a man's good parts.

If the archangel Gabriel were to come down to earth and mix in human affairs, I believe his character would be assailed within forty-eight hours. Slander called Christ a gluttonous man and a winebibber. He claimed to be the Truth, but instead of worshipping Him, men took Him and crucified Him.

When anyone spoke evil of another in the presence of Peter the Great, he would promptly stop him and say, "Well, now, has he not got a bright side? Tell me what you know good of him. It is easy to splash mud, but I would rather help a man to keep his coat clean."

I don't need to run through the whole catalog of sins that are related to these three. False rumor, exaggeration, misrepresentation, insinuation, gossip, equivocation, holding truth back when it is due and right to tell it, disparagement, and perversion of meaning – these are common transgressions of this ninth commandment, differing in form and degree of guilt according to the motive or manner of their expression. They bear false witness against a man before the tribunal of public opinion – a court whose judgment none of us escape. Since much of our life is lived in public view, any untruth that leads to a false judgment is a grievous wrong.

A Test of True Religion

Government of the tongue is made the test of true religion by James. *If anyone thinks himself to be religious, and yet does not bridle his tongue but deceives his own heart, this man's religion is worthless. For we all stumble in many ways. If anyone does not stumble in what he says, he is a perfect man, able to bridle the whole body as well* (James 1:26; 3:2). Just as a doctor looks at the tongue and can tell the condition of the body's health, so a man's words are an index of what is within. Truth will spring from a good heart; falsehood and deceit from a corrupt heart. When Ananias kept back part of the price of the land, Peter asked him, *why has Satan filled your heart to lie to the Holy Spirit?* (Acts 5:3). Satan is the father of lies and the promoter of lies.

For Good or Evil

The tongue can be an instrument of untold good or incalculable evil. Someone has said that a sharp tongue is the only edged tool that grows keener with constant use. *Your tongue devises destruction, like a sharp razor, O worker of deceit* (Psalm 52:2). *They sharpen their tongues as a serpent; Poison of a viper is under their lips* (Psalm 140:3). *The mouth of the righteous is a fountain of life, but the mouth of the wicked conceals violence* (Proverbs 10:11). *A soothing tongue is a tree of life, but perversion in it crushes the spirit* (Proverbs 15:4). Bishop Hall said that the tongues of busybodies are like the tails of Samson's foxes – they carry firebrands and are enough to set the whole field of the world in a flame.

> *Now if we put the bits into the horses' mouths so that they will obey us, we direct their entire body as well. Look at the ships also, though they are so great and are driven by strong winds, are still directed by a very small rudder*

wherever the inclination of the pilot desires.
So also the tongue is a small part of the body,
and yet it boasts of great things. See how great
a forest is set aflame by such a small fire! And
the tongue is a fire, the very world of iniquity;
the tongue is set among our members as that
which defiles the entire body, and sets on fire
the course of our life, and is set on fire by hell.
For every species of beasts and birds, of reptiles
and creatures of the sea, is tamed and has been
tamed by the human race. But no one can tame
the tongue; it is a restless evil and full of deadly
poison. With it we bless our Lord and Father,
and with it we curse men, who have been made
in the likeness of God; from the same mouth
come both blessing and cursing. My brethren,
these things ought not to be this way. Does a
fountain send out from the same opening both
fresh and bitter water? Can a fig tree, my breth-
ren, produce olives, or a vine produce figs? Nor
can salt water produce fresh. Who among you
is wise and understanding? Let him show by
his good behavior his deeds in the gentleness
of wisdom. But if you have bitter jealousy and
selfish ambition in your heart, do not be arro-
gant and so lie against the truth. (James 3:3-14)

Blighted hopes and blasted reputations are witness to
the tongue's awful power. In many cases the tongue has
murdered its victims. Can't we all recall cases where men

and women have died from the wounds of falsehoods and misrepresentation? History is full of such cases.

Permanence of Words

The most dangerous thing about speaking is that once a word is uttered, it can never be obliterated. Someone has said that lying is worse than counterfeiting. There is some hope of locating bad coins until they are all recovered, but an evil word can never be removed. The mind of the hearer or reader has been poisoned, and human devices cannot reach in and cleanse it. Lies can never be called back.

> The most dangerous thing about speaking is that once a word is uttered, it can never be obliterated.

A woman who was well known as a gossiper went and confessed to the priest. He gave her the top of a thistle and told her to go out and scatter the seeds one by one. She wondered at the penance, but obeyed; then she came and told the priest. Next, he told her to go and gather the scattered seeds. Of course, she saw that it was impossible. The priest used this as an object lesson to cure her of the sin of scandalous talk.

The Fate of the Liar and Slanderer

These sins are devilish, and the Bible is severe in its condemnation of them. It contains many solemn warnings. *You destroy those who speak falsehood; The LORD abhors the man of bloodshed and deceit* (Psalm 5:6). *The mouths of those who speak lies will be stopped* (Psalm 63:11). *Whoever secretly slanders his neighbor, him I will destroy* (Psalm 101:5). *Lying lips are an abomination to the LORD, but those who deal faithfully are His delight* (Proverbs 12:22). *For by your words you will be justified, and by your words you will be condemned* (Matthew 12:37). *For all liars, their part will be in the lake that burns with fire and brimstone, which is the second death* (Revelation 21:8). *Everyone who loves and practices lying* shall in no wise enter into the new Jerusalem (Revelation 22:15).

How to Overcome

"But, Mr. Moody," you say, "how can I change? How can I overcome the habit of lying and gossip?" A lady once told me that she had such a habit of exaggerating that her friends said they could never believe her.

The cure is simple but not very pleasant. Treat it as a sin and confess it to God and the person you have wronged. As soon as you catch yourself lying, go straight to the person and confess you have lied. Let your confession be as large as your transgression. If you have slandered or lied about anyone in public, let your confession be public. Many people say some mean, false thing about another in the presence of others and then try to patch it up by going to that person alone. That is not making restitution. I need not go to God with confession until I have made it right with that person, if it is in my power to do so.

Hannah Moore's method was a sure cure for gossip. Whenever she was told anything derogatory about another, invariably her reply was, "Come, we will go and ask if it is true."

The effect was sometimes ludicrously painful. The talebearer was surprised, stammered out a qualification, or begged that no notice be taken of the statement. But the good lady was unyielding. Off she took the gossiper to the scandalized person to inquire and compare accounts.

It is not likely that anybody ventured a second time to repeat a gossipy story to Hannah Moore.

My friend, how is it? If God should weigh you against this commandment, would you be found wanting? *You shall not bear false witness.* Are you innocent or guilty?

Chapter 10

The Tenth Commandment

You shall not covet your neighbor's house;
you shall not covet your neighbor's wife or
his male servant or his female servant or his
ox or his donkey or anything that belongs to
your neighbor. (Exodus 20:17)

I n the twelfth chapter of Luke, our Savior lifted two danger signals. *Beware of the leaven of the Pharisees, which is hypocrisy. Be on your guard against every form of greed* (Luke 12:1, 15).

The greatest dupe the devil has in the world is the hypocrite, but the next greatest is the covetous man, *for not even when one has an abundance does his life consist of his possessions* (Luke 12:15).

I believe this sin is more prevalent now than ever before in the world's history. We are not in the habit of condemning it as a sin. In his first epistle to the Thessalonians, Paul speaks of *a cloke of covetousness*

(1 Thessalonians 2:5 KJV). Covetous men use their covetousness as a cloak and call it frugality and foresight. Who ever heard it confessed as a sin? I have heard many confessions, in public and private, during the past forty years, but never have I heard a man confess that he was guilty of this sin. The Bible does not tell of one man who ever recovered from it, and in all my experience, I do not recall many who have been able to get rid of it after it had ensnared them. A covetous man or woman generally remains covetous to the very end.

We may say that covetous desire plunged the human race into sin. We can trace the river back from age to age until we get to its origin in Eden. When Eve saw that the forbidden fruit was good for food and that it was desirable to the eyes, she partook of it and Adam with her. They were not satisfied with all that God had showered upon them but coveted the wisdom of gods which Satan deceitfully told them would be obtained by eating the fruit. She saw, she desired, then she took! Three steps from innocence into sin.

Our innermost life, invisible to the mortal eye, is laid bare before Him.

A Searching Commandment

It would be absurd for such a law as this to be placed upon any human statute book. It could never be enforced. The officers of the law would be powerless to detect infractions. The outward conduct may be regulated, but the thoughts and intents of a man are beyond the reach of human law.

But God can see behind outward actions. He can

read the thoughts of the heart. Our innermost life, invisible to the mortal eye, is laid bare before Him. We cannot deceive Him by external conformity. He is able to detect the least transgression and shortcoming, so that no man can shirk detection. God is not misled by the cleanness of the outside of the cup and the platter.

Surely, we have here another proof that the Ten Commandments are not of human origin but must be divine. This commandment did not even on the surface confine itself to visible actions as did the preceding commandments. Even before Christ came and showed the breadth of their spiritual span, men had a commandment that went beyond public conduct and touched the very motivations of action. It directly prohibited not the wrong act, but the wicked desire that prompted the act. It forbade the evil thought, the unlawful wish. It sought to prevent not only sin but also the desire to sin. In God's sight, it is as wicked to set covetous eyes upon anything that is not ours as it is to lay thieving hands on it.

And why? Because if the evil desire can be controlled, there will be no failure in conduct. Desires have been called "actions in the egg." The desire in the heart is the first step in the series that ends in action. Kill the evil desire, and you successfully avoid the ill results that would follow upon its hatching and development. Prevention is better than cure.

We must not limit covetousness to the matter of money. The commandment is not limited in that way; it reads, *You shall not covet . . . anything.* That word *anything* is what will condemn us. Though we do not join in the race for wealth, don't we sometimes have a hungry longing for our neighbors' good lands, fine houses, beautiful clothes, brilliant reputation, personal accomplishments, easy circumstances, and comfortable surroundings? Haven't we had the desire to increase our possessions or change our standard of living in accordance with what we see in others? If so, we are guilty of having broken this law.

God's Thoughts about Covetousness

Let's examine a few of the Bible passages that focus on this sin and see what God's thoughts are about it.

> *Or do you not know that the unrighteous will not inherit the kingdom of God? Do not be deceived; neither fornicators, nor idolaters, nor adulterers, nor effeminate, nor homosexuals, nor thieves, nor the covetous, nor drunkards, nor revilers, nor swindlers, will inherit the kingdom of God.*
> (1 Corinthians 6:9-10)

Notice that the covetous are named between thieves and drunkards. We lock up thieves and have no mercy on them. We loathe drunkards and consider them great sinners against the law of God as well as the law of the land. Yet there is much more said in the Bible against covetousness than against either stealing or drunkenness.

Covetousness and stealing are almost like Siamese twins – they often go together. In fact, we might add lying to them and make them a triplet. "The covetous person is a thief *in* the shell. The thief is a covetous person *out of* the shell. Let a covetous person see something that he desires very much; let an opportunity of taking it be offered; how very soon, like the chicken ready to be hatched, he will break through the shell and come out in his true character as a thief."[13] The Greek word translated *covetousness* means "an inordinate desire of getting." When the Gauls tasted the sweet wines of Italy, they asked where they came from and never rested until they had overrun Italy.

> *For this you know with certainty, that no*
> *immoral or impure person or covetous man,*
> *who is an idolater, has an inheritance in the*
> *kingdom of Christ and God.* (Ephesians 5:5)

There we have the same truth repeated, but notice that covetousness is called idolatry. The covetous man worships mammon, not God.

> *Furthermore, you shall select out of all*
> *the people able men who fear God, men of*
> *truth, those who* **hate dishonest gain***, and*
> *you shall place these over them as leaders*
> *of thousands, of hundreds, of fifties and of*
> *tens.* (Exodus 18:21, author's emphasis)

Isn't it extraordinary that Jethro, the man of the desert, should have given this advice to Moses? How did he learn to beware of covetousness? We honor men today if they are wealthy and covetous. We elect them to office in church and state. We often say that they will

---

13   Richard Newton, *The King's Highway; or, Illustrations of the Commandments* (London: Thomas Nelson and Sons, Paternoster Row, 1861), 257.

make better treasurers just because we know they are covetous. But in God's sight, a covetous man is as vile and black as any thief or drunkard. David said, *For the wicked boasts of his heart's desire, and the greedy man curses and spurns the LORD* (Psalm 10:3). I am afraid that many who profess to have put away wickedness also speak well of the covetous.

A Sore Evil

> *He who loves money will not be satisfied with money, nor he who loves abundance with its income. This too is vanity. When good things increase, those who consume them increase. So what is the advantage to their owners except to look on? The sleep of the working man is pleasant, whether he eats little or much; but the full stomach of the rich man does not allow him to sleep. There is a grievous evil which I have seen under the sun: riches being hoarded by their owner to his hurt.* (Ecclesiastes 5:10-13)

Isn't that true? Is the covetous man ever satisfied with his possessions? Aren't they vanity? Does he have peace of mind? Don't selfish riches always bring hurt?

The folly of covetousness is shown in the following extract:

> If you should see a man that had a large pond of water, yet living in continual thirst, not suffering himself to drink half a draught, for fear of lessening his pond;

if you should see him wasting his time
and strength in fetching more water to his
pond, always thirsty, yet always carrying a
bucket of water in his hand, watching early
and late to catch the drops of rain, gaping
after every cloud, and running greedily into
every mire and mud, in hopes of water, and
always studying how to make every ditch
empty itself into the pond: if you should
see him grow grey and old in these anxious
labours, and at last end a careful, thirsty
life, by falling into his own pond; would
you not say that such a one was not only the
author of his own disquiets, but was foolish
enough to be reckoned amongst idiots and
madmen? But yet foolish and absurd as this
character is, it does not represent half the
follies, and absurd disquiets, of the covetous man.[14]

I have read of a millionaire in France who was a miser.
In order to secure his wealth, he dug a cave in his wine
cellar so large and deep that he needed a ladder to go
down into it. The entrance had a door with a spring
lock. After a time, he went missing. A search was made,
but they could find no trace of him. At last, his house
was sold, and the purchaser discovered this door in the
cellar. He opened it, went down, and found the miser
lying dead on the ground in the midst of his riches.

---

14   William Law, *A Serious Call to a Devout and Holy Life* (Newcastle:
      J. Barker, Hood Street, 1845), 106.

The door must have shut accidentally after him, and he perished miserably.

A Temptation and a Snare

But those who want to get rich fall into temptation and a snare and many foolish and harmful desires which plunge men into ruin and destruction. (1 Timothy 6:9)

The Bible speaks of the deceitfulness of two things – *the deceitfulness of sin* and *the deceitfulness of riches* (Hebrews 3:13; Mark 4:19). Riches are like a mirage in the desert, which has all the appearance of satisfying, and lures the traveler with the promise of water and shade, but he only wastes his strength in the effort to reach it. Likewise, riches never satisfy; the pursuit of them is always an entrapment.

> Riches never satisfy; the pursuit of them is always an entrapment.

Lot coveted the rich plains of Sodom, and what did he gain? After twenty years spent in that wicked city, he had to escape for his life, leaving all his wealth behind him.

What did the thirty pieces of silver do for Judas (Matthew 26:15; 27:3)? Weren't they a snare?

Think of Balaam. He is generally regarded as a false prophet, but I do not find that any of his prophecies that are recorded are not true; they have been literally fulfilled. Up to a certain point, his character shone magnificently, but the devil finally overcame him through covetousness. He stepped over a heavenly crown for the riches and honors that Balak promised him (Numbers 22:37; Jude 11). His face was set toward God, but he backed into hell. He wanted to die the death of the righteous, but he did not live the life of the righteous. It is sad to see so many who know God but miss everything for riches.

Then consider the case of Gehazi, who was drowned in destruction and perdition by covetousness. He got more from Naaman than he asked for, but he also got Naaman's leprosy. Think how he forfeited the friendship of his master, Elisha, the man of God:

> But Gehazi, the servant of Elisha the man of God, thought, "Behold, my master has spared this Naaman the Aramean, by not receiving from his hands what he brought. As the LORD lives, I will run after him and take something from him."
>
> So Gehazi pursued Naaman. When Naaman saw one running after him, he came down from the chariot to meet him and said, "Is all well?"
>
> He said, "All is well. My master has sent me, saying, 'Behold, just now two young men of the sons of the prophets have come to me from the hill country of Ephraim. Please give them a talent of silver and two changes of clothes.' "
>
> Naaman said, "Be pleased to take two talents." And he urged him, and bound two talents of silver in two bags with two changes of

clothes and gave them to two of his servants;
and they carried them before him.

When he came to the hill, he took them from
their hand and deposited them in the house,
and he sent the men away, and they departed.

But he went in and stood before his master.
And Elisha said to him, "Where have you
been, Gehazi?" And he said, "Your servant
went nowhere."

Then he said to him, "Did not my heart go
with you, when the man turned from his
chariot to meet you? Is it a time to receive
money and to receive clothes and olive groves
and vineyards and sheep and oxen and male
and female servants?"

"Therefore, the leprosy of Naaman shall cling
to you and to your descendants forever." So he
went out from his presence a leper as white as
snow. (2 Kings 5:20-27)

So today, lifelong friends are separated by this accursed desire. Homes are broken up. Men are willing to sell their peace and happiness for the sake of a few dollars.

Didn't David fall into foolish and hurtful lusts? He saw Bathsheba, Uriah's wife, and she *was very beautiful in appearance*, and David became a murderer and an adulterer (2 Samuel 11). The guilty longing hurled him into the deepest pit of sin. He had to reap bitterly as he had sowed.

I heard of a wealthy German out west who owned a lumber mill. He was worth nearly two million dollars, but his covetousness was so great that he once worked as a common laborer carrying railroad ties all day. It was the cause of his death.

> *So Achan answered Joshua and said,*
> *"Truly, I have sinned against the LORD, the*
> *God of Israel, and this is what I did: when*
> *I saw among the spoil a beautiful mantle*
> *from Shinar and two hundred shekels*
> *of silver and a bar of gold fifty shekels in*
> *weight, then I coveted them and took them;*
> *and behold, they are concealed in the earth*
> *inside my tent with the silver underneath*
> *it." (Joshua 7:20-21)*

He saw, he coveted, he took, and he hid! The covetous eye was what led Achan to the wicked deed that brought sorrow and defeat upon the camp of Israel.

We know the terrible punishment that was meted out to Achan. They stoned and burned him and his family and his livestock (Joshua 7:24-25). God seems to have set danger signals at the threshold of each new age. It is remarkable how soon the first outbreaks of covetousness occurred. Think of Eve in Eden or Achan just after Israel had entered the promised land, and Ananias and Sapphira in the early Christian church.

A Root Extractor

> *For the love of money is a root of all sorts*
> *of evil, and some by longing for it have*

> *wandered away from the faith and pierced*
> *themselves with many griefs.* (1 Timothy 6:10)

The Revised Version translates it – *a root of all kinds of evil*. This tenth commandment has therefore been aptly called a "root-extractor," because it would tear up and destroy this root. Deep down in our corrupt nature, covetousness has spread. No one but God can rid us of it.

Matthew tells us that the deceitfulness of riches chokes the Word of God, like the Mississippi River chokes up its mouth by the amount of soil it carries and deposits at its end. Isn't that true of many businessmen today? They are so engrossed with their affairs that they don't have time for religion. They lose sight of their soul and its eternal welfare in their desire to amass wealth. They do not even hesitate to sell their souls to the devil. How many men have said, "We must make money, and if God's law stands in the way, brush it aside."

Greed for gold leads men to commit violence and murder, to cheat and deceive and steal.

The word *lucre* occurs five times in the King James New Testament, and each time it is called *filthy* lucre.

A root of all kinds of evil. Yes, because what will men not be guilty of when prompted by the desire to be rich? Greed for gold leads men to commit violence and murder, to cheat and deceive and steal. It turns the heart to stone, devoid of all natural affection, cruel and unkind. How many families are wrecked over the father's desires! The scramble for a share of the wealth smashes them to pieces. Bodily health is no consideration. The uncontrollable fever for gold makes men turn from secure work and undertake hazardous journeys; no danger can drive them back. It destroys faith and spirituality, turning men's minds and hearts away from God. It disturbs the peace of the community by encouraging wrongful acts. Covetousness has more than once led nation to war against nation for the sake of gaining territory or other material resources. It is said that when the Spaniards came over to conquer Peru, they sent a message to the king, saying, "Give us gold, for we Spaniards have a disease that can only be cured by gold."

Dr. Boardman has shown how covetousness leads to the transgression of every one of the commandments, and I cannot do better than quote his words:

> Coveting tempts us into the violation of the First Commandment, or polytheism, worshiping Mammon in addition to Jehovah. . . . Coveting tempts us into a violation of the Second Commandment, or idolatry. . . . The Apostle Paul expressly identifies the covetous man and the idolater: "Covetousness, the which is idolatry." Again: Coveting tempts us into violation of the Third Commandment, or sacrilegious falsehood: for instance, Gehazi, lying in the matter of his interview with Naaman the Syrian, and Ananias and Sapphira, perjuring themselves in the matter of the community of goods. Again: Coveting

tempts us into violation of the Fourth
Commandment, or Sabbath-breaking; it is
covetousness which encroaches on God's
appointed day of sacred rest, tempting us to
run trains for merely secular purposes, to
vend tobacco and liquors, to hawk newspapers. Again: Coveting tempts us into violation of the Fifth Commandment, or disrespect for authority; tempting the young man
to deride his early parental counsels, the citi-
zen to trample on civic enactments. Again:
Covetousness tempts us into violation of the
Sixth Commandment, or murder; recall how
Judas' love of money lured him into the sac-
rilegious betrayal of his Divine Friend into
the hand of his murderers, his lure being the
paltry sum of – say – fifteen dollars. Again:
Covetousness tempts us into violation of
the Seventh Commandment, or adultery;
observe how Scripture combines greed and
lust . . . Again: Covetousness tempts us into
violation of the Eighth Commandment, or
theft; recall how it tempted Achan to steal a
goodly Babylonish mantle, and two hundred shekels of silver, and a wedge of gold
of fifty shekels weight. Again: Covetousness
tempts us into violation of the Ninth
Commandment, or bearing false witness
against our neighbor; recall how the covetousness of Ahab instigated his wife Jezebel
to employ sons of Belial to bear blasphemous

and fatal testimony against Naboth, saying, "Thou didst curse God and the king."[15]

How to Overcome

You ask me how you are to cast this unclean spirit out of your heart? I think I can tell you.

In the first place, make up your mind that by the grace of God you will overcome the spirit of selfishness. You must overcome it, or it will overcome you. Paul said, *Therefore consider the members of your earthly body as dead to immorality, impurity, passion, evil desire, and greed, which amounts to idolatry. For it is because of these things that the wrath of God will come upon the sons of disobedience* (Colossians 3:5-6).

I heard of a rich man who was asked to contribute to a charitable project. The text was quoted to him: *One who is gracious to a poor man lends to the LORD, and He will repay him for his good deed* (Proverbs 19:17). He said that the security might be good enough, but the credit was for too long. He was dead within two weeks. The wrath of God rested upon him as he never expected.

If you find yourself getting miserly, give abundantly like a wealthy farmer in New York State I heard of. He was a noted miser, but he was converted. Soon after, a poor man who had been burned out and had no provisions came to him for help. The farmer thought he would be liberal and give the man a ham from his

---

15   George Dana Boardman, *The Ten Commandments* (Philadelphia: American Baptist Publication Society, 1889), 315-316.

smokehouse. On his way to get it, the tempter whispered to him, "Give him the smallest one you have."

He had a struggle as to whether he would give a large or a small ham, but finally he took down the largest he could find.

"You are a fool," the devil said.

"If you don't keep still," the farmer replied, "I will give him every ham I have in the smokehouse."

Mr. Durant told me he woke up one morning to find that he was a rich man, and he said the greatest struggle of his life then took place as to whether he would let money be his master or he be the master of his money – whether he would be its slave or make it a slave to him. At last, he got the victory, and that was how Wellesley College came to be built.

Next, one must cultivate the spirit of contentment. *Make sure that your character is free from the love of money, being content with what you have; for He Himself has said, "I will never desert you, nor will I ever forsake you," so that we confidently say, "The Lord is my helper, I will not be afraid. What will man do to me* (Hebrews 13:5-6)?"

Contentment is the very opposite of covetousness, which is continually craving for something you do not possess. Be content with such things as ye have, not worrying about the future, because God has promised never to leave you or forsake you. What does the child of God want more than this? I would rather have that promise than all the gold of the earth.

I wish we might all be able to say with Paul: *I have coveted no one's silver or gold or clothes* (Acts 20:33).

The Lord had made him a partaker of His grace, and he was soon to be a partaker of His glory, and earthly things looked very small. *Godliness actually is a means of great gain when accompanied by contentment*, he wrote to Timothy; *if we have food and covering, with these we shall be content* (1 Timothy 6:6, 8).

No worldly gain can satisfy the human heart.

Observe that he puts godliness first. No worldly gain can satisfy the human heart. If we could gain the whole world, there would still be room in the heart.

May God tear the scales from our eyes if we are blinded by this sin. Oh, the folly of it, that we should set our heart's affections upon anything below! *For we have brought nothing into the world, so we cannot take anything out of it either* (1 Timothy 6:7). *Do not be afraid when a man becomes rich, when the glory of his house is increased; For when he dies he will carry nothing away; His glory will not descend after him* (Psalm 49:16-17).

Blotted-Out Handwriting

We have now considered the Ten Commandments, and the question for each one of us is, are we keeping them? If God should weigh us by them, would we be found wanting or not wanting? Do we keep the law, the whole law? Are we obeying God with all our heart? Do we render Him a full and willing obedience?

Chapter 11

One Law, Not Ten

These Ten Commandments are not ten different laws; they are one law. If I am being held up in the air by a chain with ten links and I break one of them, down I come, just as surely as if I break all ten. If I am forbidden to go out of an enclosure, it makes no difference at what point I break through the fence. *For whoever keeps the whole law and yet stumbles in one point, he has become guilty of all* (James 2:10). The golden chain of obedience is broken if one link is missing.

We sometimes hear people pray to be preserved from certain sins, as if they were in no danger of committing others. I firmly believe that if a man begins by willfully breaking one of these commandments, it is much easier then for him to break the others. I know of a gentleman who had a confidential clerk and insisted on him working on the books on Sunday morning. The young man had a good deal of principle and at first refused, but he was anxious to stay in the good graces of his employer and finally yielded. Before long, he speculated in stocks and became a defaulter for $120,000. The employer had him arrested and put in the penitentiary for ten years, but I believe he was just as guilty in the sight of God as that young man, for he led him to take the first step on the downward road. You remember the story of a soldier who was smuggled into a fortress in a load of hay and opened the gates to his comrades. Every sin we commit opens the door for other sins.

All Have Come Short

For fifteen hundred years, man was under the law, and no one could live up to it. Christ came and showed that the commandments went beyond the mere letter. Can anyone since then say that he has been able to keep them in his own strength? As the plumb line is held up, we see how much we are out of the perpendicular – how far we have strayed. As we measure ourselves by that holy standard, we find how much we are lacking. As a child said, when reproved by her mother and told that she ought to do right, "How can I do right when there is no 'right' in me?" *There is none righteous, not even one; for all have sinned and fall short of the glory of God* (Romans 3:10, 23).

> Every sin we commit opens the door for other sins.

I do not say that all are equally guilty of gross violations of the commandments. It needs a certain amount of reckless courage to openly break a law, human or divine; but it is easy to *crack* the commandments, as a child once said. It has been stated that the lives of many professors of religion are full of fractures that result from little sins, little acts of temper and selfishness. It is possible to crack a costly vase so finely that it cannot be noticed by the observer, but if this is done again and again in different directions, someday the vase will crumble to pieces at a touch. When we hear of someone who has had a lifelong reputation for good character and consistent living, and who suddenly falls into some shameful sin, we are shocked and puzzled. If we knew everything, we would find that only the fall has been sudden. He has been sliding toward it for years. Long ago in his life, we would find numerous *cracked* commandments. His exposure is only the falling of the vase to pieces.

False Weights

Men have all sorts of weights that they think are going to satisfy them, but they will find that they are altogether vanity and lighter than vanity.

The moral man is as guilty as the rest. His morality cannot save him. *Unless you repent, you will all likewise perish* (Luke 13:3). *Unless you are converted and become like children, you will not enter the kingdom of heaven* (Matthew 18:3). I have often heard good people say that our meetings were doing good; they were reaching the drunkards and gamblers and harlots, but they never realized that they needed the grace of God for themselves.

Nicodemus was probably one of the most moral men of his day. He was a teacher of the law. Yet Christ said to him, *Unless one is born again he cannot see the kingdom of God* (John 3:3). It is much easier to reach thieves and drunkards and vagabonds than self-righteous Pharisees. You do not have to preach to those men for weeks and months to convince them that they are sinners. When a man learns that he needs God and that he is a sinner, it is very easy to reach him. But the self-righteous Pharisee needs salvation as much as any drunkard that walks the streets.

I read of a minister traveling in the South who obtained permission to preach in the local jail. A son of his host went with him. On the way back, the young man, who was not a Christian, said to the minister, "I hope some of the convicts were impressed. Such a sermon as that ought to do them good."

"Did it do you good?" the minister asked.

"Oh, you were preaching to the convicts!" the young man answered.

The minister shook his head and said, "I preached Christ, and you need Him as much as they do."

If you do not repent of your sins and ask Him for mercy, there is no hope for you. Let me ask you to take this question to your own heart. If a summons should come at midnight for you to be *weighed in the balances*, what would become of your soul?

Many are only making a profession of faith. You belong to the church, but are you ready to be weighed? Ready to step on the scales? A great many would be found like those five foolish virgins. When the hour came, they would be found with no oil in their lamps (Matthew 25:1-13). If you only have an empty lamp or are living on mere legalism, I beg of you to give it up. Give up that dead, cold, miserable lukewarmness. God will have none of it. Are you trusting your good works? Do you think your Bible, your cross, your prayers, or your church-going will help you?

Or do you set your hope on your education, your wealth, or your earthly distinctions? What will your university education amount to and all your wealth and honors, if you succumb to lust and passion and covetousness, and lose your soul in the end? We are not redeemed *with perishable things like silver or gold, but with precious blood... the blood of Christ* (1 Peter 1:18-19). If you don't have Christ when God weighs you, *Tekel* will be your sentence.

Do Not Despair

I can imagine that you are saying to yourself, "If we are to be judged by these laws, how are we going to be saved? Nearly every one of them has been broken by us – in spirit, if not in letter." I almost hear you say, "I wonder if Mr. Moody is ready to be weighed. Would he like to put those tests to himself?"

With all humility, I reply that if God commanded me to step on the scales now, I am ready.

"What!" you say. "Haven't you broken the law?"

Yes, I have. I was a sinner before God the same as you, but forty years ago I pled guilty at His court. I cried for mercy, and He forgave me. If I step on the scales, the Son of God has promised to be with me. I would not dare to step on them without Him. If I did, the scales would quickly fly up!

Christ Is All

Christ kept the law. If He had ever broken it, He would have had to die for Himself. But because He was a Lamb without spot or blemish, His atoning death is effective for you and me. He had no sin of His own to atone for, so God accepted His sacrifice for us. *For Christ is the end of the law for righteousness to everyone who believes* (Romans 10:4). We are righteous in God's sight because the righteousness of God that is by faith in Jesus Christ is unto all and upon all who believe.

If we had to live forever with our sins in the handwriting of God on the wall, it would be hell on earth. But thank God for the gospel we preach! If we repent, our sins will all be blotted out. *When you were dead in your transgressions and the uncircumcision of your flesh, He made you alive together with Him, having forgiven us all our transgressions, having canceled out the certificate of debt consisting of decrees* [handwriting of ordinances] *against us, which was hostile to us; and He has taken it out of the way, having nailed it to the cross* (Colossians 2:13-14).

The Fulfilling of the Law

If the love of God is shed abroad in your heart, you will be able to fulfill the law. Paul reduced the commandments to one: *Love is the fulfillment of the law* (Romans 13:10). An unknown author has written the following restatement of the Ten Commandments:

Love to God will admit no other God.

Love resents everything that debases its
object by representing it by an image.

Love to God will never dishonor His name.

Love to God will reverence His day.

Love to parents makes one honor them.

Hate, not love, is a murderer.

Lust, not love, commits adultery.

Love will give, but never steal.

Love will not slander or lie.

Love's eye is not covetous.

Are You Ready?

It is the height of madness to turn from God and run
the risk of being called by Him to judgment with no
hope in Christ. Now is the day and hour to accept salvation, and then He will be with you. Do you step aside
and say, "I'm not ready yet. I want a little more time to
prepare, to turn the matter over in my mind"? Well,
you have time, but bear in mind it is only the present;
you do not know that you will have tomorrow.

Wasn't Belshazzar cut off suddenly? Would he have
believed that that was going to be his last night, that he
would never see the light of another sun? That banquet
of sin didn't end as he expected. As long as you delay,
you are in danger. If you don't enter into the kingdom

of heaven by God's way, you cannot enter at all. You must accept Christ as your Savior, or you will never be fit to be weighed.

My friend, do you have Him? Will you remain as you are and be found wanting, or will you accept Christ and be ready for the summons? *And the testimony is this, that God has given us eternal life, and this life is in His Son. He who has the Son has the life; he who does not have the Son of God does not have the life* (1 John 5:11-12).

May God open your heart to receive His Son now!

Dwight L. Moody –
A Brief Biography

Dwight Lyman Moody was born on February 5, 1837, in Northfield, Massachusetts. His father died when Dwight was only four years old, leaving his mother with nine children to care for. When Dwight was seventeen years old, he left for Boston to work as a salesman. A year later, he was led to Jesus Christ by Edward Kimball, Moody's Sunday school teacher. Moody soon left for Chicago and began teaching a Sunday school class of his own. By the time he was twenty-three, he had become a successful shoe salesman, earing $5,000 in only eight months, which was a lot of money for the middle of the nineteenth century. Having decided to follow Jesus, though, he left his career to engage in Christian work for only $300 a year.

D. L. Moody was not an ordained minister, but was an effective evangelist. He was once told by Henry Varley, a British evangelist, "Moody, the world has yet to see what God will do with a man fully consecrated to Him."

Moody later said, "By God's help, I aim to be that man."

It is estimated that during his lifetime, without the help of television or radio, Moody traveled more than one million miles, preached to more than one million people, and personally dealt with over seven hundred and fifty thousand individuals.

D. L. Moody died on December 22, 1899.

Moody once said, "Some day you will read in the papers that D. L. Moody, of East Northfield, is dead. Don't you believe a word of it! At that moment I shall be more alive than I am now. I shall have gone up higher, that is all – out of this old clay tenement into a house that is immortal; a body that death cannot touch, that sin cannot taint, a body fashioned like unto His glorious body. I was born of the flesh in 1837. I was born of the Spirit in 1856. That which is born of the flesh may die. That which is born of the Spirit will live forever."

Similar Updated Classics

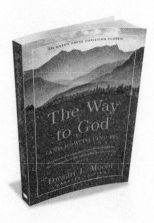

The Way to God, by Dwight L. Moody

There is life in Christ. Rich, joyous, wonderful life. It is true that the Lord disciplines those whom He loves and that we are often tempted by the world and our enemy, the devil. But if we know how to go beyond that temptation to cling to the cross of Jesus Christ and keep our eyes on our Lord, our reward both here on earth and in heaven will be 100 times better than what this world has to offer.

This book is thorough. It brings to life the love of God, examines the state of the unsaved individual's soul, and analyzes what took place on the cross for our sins. *The Way to God* takes an honest look at our need to repent and follow Jesus, and gives hope for unending, joyous eternity in heaven.

Available where books are sold.

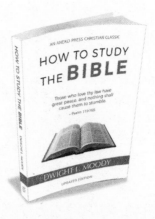

How to Study the Bible,
by Dwight L. Moody

There is no situation in life for which you cannot find some word of consolation in Scripture. If you are in affliction, if you are in adversity and trial, there is a promise for you. In joy and sorrow, in health and in sickness, in poverty and in riches, in every condition of life, God has a promise stored up in His Word for you.

This classic book by Dwight L. Moody brings to light the necessity of studying the Scriptures, presents methods which help stimulate excitement for the Scriptures, and offers tools to help you comprehend the difficult passages in the Scriptures. To live a victorious Christian life, you must read and understand what God is saying to you. Moody is a master of using stories to illustrate what he is saying, and you will be both inspired and convicted to pursue truth from the pages of God's Word.

Available where books are sold.

The Overcoming Life, by Dwight L. Moody

Are you an overcomer? Or, are you plagued by little sins that easily beset you? Even worse, are you failing in your Christian walk, but refuse to admit and address it? No Christian can afford to dismiss the call to be an overcomer. The earthly cost is minor; the eternal reward is beyond measure.

Dwight L. Moody is a master at unearthing what ails us. He uses stories and humor to bring to light the essential principles of successful Christian living. Each aspect of overcoming is looked at from a practical and understandable angle. The solution Moody presents for our problems is not religion, rules, or other outward corrections. Instead, he takes us to the heart of the matter and prescribes biblical, God-given remedies for every Christian's life. Get ready to embrace genuine victory for today, and joy for eternity.

Available where books are sold.

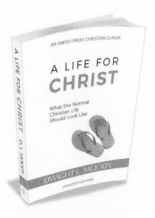

A Life for Christ, by Dwight L. Moody

In the church today, we have everything buttoned up perfectly. The music is flawless, the sermon well-prepared and smoothly delivered, and the grounds meticulously kept. People come on time and go home on time. But a fundamental element is missing. The business of church has undermined the individual's need to truly live for Christ, so much so, that only a limited few are seeing their life impact the world.

Dwight L. Moody takes us deep into Scripture and paints a clear picture of what ought to be an individual's life for Christ. The call for each Christian is to become an active member in the body of Christ. The motive is love for the Lord and our neighbor. The result will be the salvation of men, women, and children everywhere.

Available where books are sold.

Repentance, by J. C. Ryle

It is indifference that leaves people alone and allows them to go their own way. It is love, tender love, that warns them and raises the cry of alarm. The cry of "Fire! Fire!" at midnight might sometimes rudely, harshly, and unpleasantly startle a person out of his sleep, but who would complain if that cry was the means of saving his life? The words *Except you repent, you will all likewise perish* might at first seem stern and severe, but they are words of love, and they could be the means of delivering precious souls from hell.

- The nature of repentance: What is it?

- The necessity of repentance: Why is repentance needful?

- The encouragements to repentance: What is there to lead people to repent?

Available where books are sold.